MW01681004

Joyful Prayerful Thankful

Discovering Your Path to Spiritual Growth and Lasting Joy

Foreword by **Mark Sanborn**
New York Times bestselling author of *The Fred Factor*

Joyful Prayerful Thankful

Discovering Your Path to Spiritual Growth and Lasting Joy

Kevin Karschnik

Joyful • Prayerful • Thankful
Discovering Your Path to Spiritual Growth and Lasting Joy

PUBLISHED BY:
Forever Green Press
Georgetown, TX

Book design and production by Desktop Miracles
www.desktopmiracles.com

ISBN: 979-8-234-02511-1

Printed in the United States of America

First Edition: 2026

Praise for

Joyful Prayerful Thankful

"Brilliant. Insightful. Compelling. Kevin's words are nourishment for the soul. *Joyful Prayerful Thankful* is more than a book—it is a faith-based tutorial for life, woven with wisdom, transparency, and personal stories that are both inspirational and practical. You can't read it without reflecting on your own life and discovering a roadmap for living with greater joy, prayer, and thankfulness."

~Don Forrester

Executive Director

Coalition of Residential Excellence (CORE)

"In this crazy fast paced world today, *Joyful Prayerful Thankful* is a much-needed invitation to slow down and return to what matters most. Kevin writes with warmth, wisdom, and authenticity. This book is worth your time."

~Reid Ryan

President and CEO

Round Rock Express Baseball Club

& Ryan Sanders Baseball

"Beautifully written and deeply meaningful, Kevin's reflections in his book *Joyful Prayerful Thankful* offers a refreshing perspective on where true joy is found in our connection with Christ. This is the kind of message I'll carry with me and share with those who need a gentle reminder of hope."

~Cheryl Graham

Learning & Development,

Leadership Development Program Manager

7-Eleven

"*Joyful Prayerful Thankful* is a much-needed reminder to pause and focus on what truly matters. Kevin's heartfelt stories and practical wisdom demonstrate that joy, prayer, and gratitude are daily choices that can profoundly transform our experience of life. His message is clear—the goal isn't to fake positivity, but to experience real joy, meaningful connections, and gratitude that lead to a more intentional and fulfilling life. This book is encouraging, actionable, and one I'll return to whenever I need to reconnect with what matters most."

~**ANNE GRADY**

Keynote Speaker and Author of

Mind Over Matter: Harness the Power of Resilience

"The Old Testament recounts the story of King Solomon's desire for Godly wisdom. And scripture tells us he ruled for many years in that wisdom. Self-awareness is the first step towards wisdom and wisdom produces something of value. Kevin's book is filled with truths and stories based on that type of wisdom. Savor it, take your time and enjoy the truths that pour out of the pages of *Joyful Prayerful Thankful*. It is filled with practical, personal and thoughtful wisdom."

~**BILL MCALPINE**

Executive Leadership and Performance Coach

"*Joyful Prayerful Thankful* is a guide that invites you the reader to embrace and incorporate you faith as a source of peace, happiness and calmness. Through heartfelt reflections, shared stories and practical insights, you gently lead toward a deeper or renewed connection with your inner self and a more joyful, prayerful, and thankful life. A must read for those seeking simple steps to growth and success based on your values."

~**ALICIA DAVIS**

Director of Global Finance L&D

Dell Technologies

"Kevin's words spoke to my heart with both simplicity and depth. In a world that constantly pulls us toward hurry and distraction, *Joyful Prayerful Thankful* felt like a gracious call to slow down and lean into what truly matters: not chasing achievement, but aligning with the One who gives our life purpose. Kevin writes with such warmth and authenticity that it feels less like reading a book and more like sitting across from a trusted friend. His stories and insights are practical and encouraging, pointing us toward a life of purpose, peace, and lasting fulfillment."

~**DR. DAVID W. SMITH**

Executive Director

Austin Baptist Association

"Blending timeless wisdom with modern relevance, Karschnik draws on performance psychology, research, and parable-style storytelling to show how joy, prayer, and gratitude are not just spiritual practices, but essential skills for thriving in both life and work. Highly recommend the read for all phases of life!"

~**DR. LAUREN HODGES**

Keynote Speaker, Author of

Less Stress, More Calm: Discover Your Unique Stress Personality and Make It Your Superpower

"In a world where the problems of the day are constantly pushed in front of us, it's easy to overlook the countless things that are going right. *Joyful Prayerful Thankful* offers a way to cut through the noise, refocus on the positive, and rediscover just how amazing your life truly is."

~**RUSS BOLES**

County Commissioner

Williamson County

"Thought-provoking, enlightening, and actionable. Kevin has nailed it again in *Joyful Prayerful Thankful.* His warmth and wisdom lights a righteous path for all to follow."

~**Brian Thomson**

Manager, Learning & Development, CMC

"*Joyful Prayerful Thankful* is a must-read. Kevin pours decades of professional experience, personal growth, and a deep commitment to helping others into every chapter. His wisdom is both practical and inspiring, offering readers a roadmap to embrace a growth mindset rooted in gratitude and faith. He leaves a gold nugget on every page—insights that will challenge, uplift, and transform. This book is more than a read; it's a journey toward a more joyful, prayerful, and thankful life."

~**Hannah Terrell,**

Director of Libraries

Austin Public Library

"I was crazy busy and thought, I just don't have time to read *Joyful Prayerful Thankful*—and I'm going to have to let Kevin down. Then I opened the manuscript and started reading. I quickly realized that it was exactly what I needed in that moment. I couldn't put it down. Kevin's skillful writing makes the content easy to read, easy to absorb, and easy to apply. I highly recommend this book to anyone navigating a transition in their life."

~**Steve Lawton,**

Director, Dell Technologies and Author of

Head First! A Crash Course in Positivity

"Kevin's book is filled with 'aha' moments that stopped me in my tracks and invited me to reassess where I am in my own life. His words are both challenging and encouraging, pointing me back to the source of true joy. This is a book I'll return to again and again."

~**Debbie Rippstein**

President

Texas Baptist Children's Home

"Kevin has a rare gift for blending wisdom, warmth, and humility in everything he does. *Joyful Prayerful Thankful* feels like sitting down with a trusted mentor who gently reminds you what truly matters. Kevin's words have encouraged and guided me through many seasons of life and leadership, and this book is a beautiful extension of that same heart. It's a must-read for anyone seeking lasting joy and purpose."

~**Alycia Angle Anderson**

Coach, Speaker, & Perspective Shifter

To Kip & Kait

I pray you live lives that are joyful, prayerful, and thankful—
hearts filled with His Spirit, until your cups overflow.
May the message in these pages draw you closer to God —
the source of life's truest purpose.

To Tracy

I am beyond thankful for your love and support.
You've always believed in me, even when I doubted myself.
You are everything I ever prayed for in a partner
—and more than I could have imagined.
This book, like so much of my life,
is possible because of you.

Table of Contents

Foreword

We live in a world that feels hurried, distracted, and uncertain. Too many of us move through life focused on what's most urgent rather than what's most meaningful. That's why Kevin Karschnik's *Joyful Prayerful Thankful* is so timely. It calls us back to three simple yet profound truths—joy, prayer, and gratitude—that steady us and guide us when everything else feels unstable.

In my work with leaders, organizations, and individuals across the globe, I've noticed a consistent theme: the people who truly thrive are not always the smartest or the most talented. They're the ones who stay grounded in purpose and anchored in what matters most. *That is exactly what Kevin captures in these pages.*

What you'll find here is not lofty theory. It's practical. It's personal. And it's deeply rooted in wisdom and lived experience. Kevin invites us to slow down, to pause, and to realign our lives with the values God has given us. He shares stories, tools, and encouragement that don't just inspire us to think differently—they equip us to live differently.

This isn't the kind of book you read once and put on the shelf. It's a book to return to often—because it reminds us of something we all know but too easily forget: true joy, steady prayer, and everyday gratitude are not just disciplines. They are a way of life.

So as you read these pages, I encourage you to let the words sink in. Reflect on them. Implement them. And when you do, you won't just enrich your own life—you'll become a wellspring of encouragement and light for the people around you.

Joyful Prayerful Thankful is an invitation. And I believe you'll be grateful you accepted it.

~Mark Sanborn

New York Times bestselling author of

The Fred Factor

Joyful Prayerful Thankful

Discovering Your Path to Spiritual Growth and Lasting Joy

1 Thessalonians 5:16-18

"Rejoice always, pray continually,
give thanks in all circumstances;
for this is God's will for you in Christ Jesus."

Purposeful

ADJECTIVE:
Having or showing intention, determination, or resolve;
done with a clear aim or objective.

Osho (Bhagwan Shree Rajneesh)

"Each person comes into this world with a specific destiny—he has something to fulfill, some message has to be delivered, some work has to be completed. You are not here accidentally—you are here meaningfully. There is a purpose behind you."

Micah 6:8

"He has shown you, O mortal, what is good.
And what does the Lord require of you?
To act justly and to love mercy and
to walk humbly with your God."

Searching for Gold

In 1849, Billy stood knee-deep in the rushing waters of the American River, sifting through dirt and gravel in hopes of striking gold. Only months earlier, he'd left everything he knew in Chicago, traveling more than 2,000 miles to Folsom, California, to embrace the Gold Rush and become a "forty-niner." With his pick, shovel, and gold pan, he chased his dream of striking it rich.

Billy didn't know it then, but his search for gold mirrors the way many of us spend our lives searching for purpose.

Days turned into weeks, then months. All Billy had to show were pieces of quartz and fool's gold (also known as pyrite). They were shiny but worthless. He watched as some prospectors hit it big within days, celebrating their newfound wealth with fine clothes, good food, and new land. Others came and went—excited at first, but quick to leave when the work was too hard or the payoff too slow.

Billy stayed. He switched tools (first a rocker box, then a sluice box). He moved to new locations (Sutter's Mill, Placer County). He studied successful prospectors, learning how to spot the most promising places to pan for gold. And through it all, he prayed with unwavering faith, pressing on with relentless persistence. He knew the gold was there—he just needed the patience and perseverance to uncover it.

The Bible tells us in Proverbs 19:21, *"Many are the plans in a person's heart, but it is the Lord's purpose that prevails."* If we're seeking direction, this verse invites us to hold our plans loosely and stay open to God's guidance. As Jeremiah 29:11 reminds us, God's plans are to prosper us and not to harm us, to give us hope and a future. That means even the waiting seasons have purpose. Sometimes closed doors, delays, or detours, are not failures—they are redirects toward a higher calling we couldn't foresee.

Finding our purpose is a lot like panning for gold. Like Billy, we often step into new waters with big dreams and great hope, only to discover that the process takes far more persistence than we imagined. Some of us know from an early age exactly what we're meant to do—and we go for it. For example, my son Kip knew he wanted to be a financial planner after an internship the summer before his senior year of college. Kip's combination of communication skills, love for people, and a gift with numbers, helped him see his purpose clearly, and he's been pursuing his calling as a Certified Financial Planner, ever since.

Others start strong but give up when the path gets hard or unclear. Many of us begin with excitement, but when results are slow, we can grow discouraged and walk away too soon. Over the years, I've witnessed many would-be entrepreneurs who left well-paying jobs to start their own businesses—full of excitement and ambition—only to return to corporate life when the results didn't happen as quickly as they'd hoped. Most of the time, it wasn't lack of talent that stopped them—it was discouragement, when progress was slow or absent.

Then there are those of us like Billy—who keep trying new paths, new cities, new careers. Searching, refining, and learning along the way. We have a growth mindset and believe our purpose is out there, and we're willing to show up every day, faithful and patient, until we find it. My daughter Kait is a great example of this. She recently left her job as a paralegal assistant—a safe, steady career path—to become a middle school teacher and coach. She wanted more than a paycheck; she wanted to invest her time and energy into shaping young lives, helping kids grow not only in skill but in character. It was a leap of faith, one that required courage, sacrifice, and trust—but it brought her work into alignment with her passion and values. Like Kait, we sometimes hear God nudging us to take a leap of faith. Hebrews 11:8 tells us that Abraham obeyed and went, even though he did not know where he was going. Purpose often requires that kind of trust.

Most people don't walk away from their purpose all at once. It usually happens gradually—often without realizing why.

In her book *Becoming You*, Suzy Welch describes what she calls the "Four Horsemen of Values Destruction"—forces that quietly pull people away from their authentic lives and into what she calls a default life. These horsemen are expectations, expediency, economic security, and events. Expectations pressure us to live according to what others want for us. Expediency tempts us to choose what's easiest instead of what truly matters. Economic security can lead us to prioritize money over meaning. And events—life disruptions like job loss, relocation, or family changes—can knock us off course and keep us there longer than intended. When one of these forces takes over, it becomes easier to settle, quit too soon, or abandon the values we once held tightly. Recognizing which horseman is at work is often the first step toward realigning with our purpose.

So let me ask you: where do you see yourself right now? Maybe you're in a season of clarity, like Kip. Maybe you're wrestling with discouragement. Or maybe you're being nudged toward a leap of faith, like Kait—or standing knee-deep in the river, like Billy, faithfully digging and waiting. Wherever you are, God can use this season to shape you.

Our purpose isn't always a lightning bolt; it's often more like gold buried beneath the surface. It takes time, it takes trial and error, and it takes trust. The key is to try to be open to God's direction. Staying persistent. Staying prayerful. And try not to walk away too soon—we may be closer to our purpose than we think. Because, in the end, it's not just about finding gold—it's about discovering the calling God has placed within us.

Martha Beck, in her book *Finding Your Own North Star*, puts it this way: *"Your own North Star is the path you are meant to follow, and it is unique to you. When you are on it, you feel alive, authentic, and at peace—even if it's challenging."* The Bible calls this our 'calling.' Ephesians 4:1 urges us to *"live a life worthy of the calling you have received."*

Your North Star, or your God-given purpose, will not only guide your steps but will light them, giving meaning to every mile of the journey. And when we discover this, we realize that God was with us in every step of the digging, every pan of dirt, and every delay. Purpose isn't just found at the end; it's forged in the process.

"The meaning of life is to find your gift.
The purpose of life is to give it away."
—Pablo Picasso

What on Earth am I Here For?

I never really thought much about what I wanted to do with my life until my sophomore year at the University of North Texas. One afternoon, my marketing professor, Dr. Massey, asked me point-blank, "So, what are you going to do after you graduate?"

I figured "Get a job" was a pretty solid answer. He paused, then smiled and quoted Yogi Berra: *If you don't know where you're going, you might wind up somewhere else.* That line stuck with me. It was the first time I began to wrestle with questions like: What am I going to do after college? What am I going to do with my life? What on earth am I here for?

And I know I'm not alone in that. I think most of us have asked some version of the "Why am I here?" question. I've heard it echoed by countless people over the years—in moments of success, in seasons of disappointment—and everywhere in between. It's the very question posed on the cover of Rick Warren's best-selling book *The Purpose Driven Life.* It's a question that doesn't fade with age or accomplishment. If anything, it grows louder the older we get.

Later that same year, I was invited to speak to the business department as the newly elected president of the Marketing Club. I broke the ice with a dad joke about "contacts" and why you should join the club to make more of them. I was nervous and my presentation was far from polished—no one would be inviting me to join the keynote speaking circuit anytime soon—but something clicked inside me that day.

I walked away from that presentation energized. It wasn't just the thrill of being in the spotlight (although that was fun too)—it was the way the audience leaned in, the smiles, the nods, the moments of connection. That day, it clicked: I wanted to spend my life in front of people—not to chase applause, but to make a difference.

Maybe for you it's something entirely different—solving problems, coding, writing, creating, healing, organizing, coaching, designing, or leading. But when something stirs our soul or sparks our energy, we need to pause and ask questions. Why does this excite me? What does it reveal about my gifts? How might I lean into it more? Because curiosity is often the first breadcrumb God drops on the trail leading us to our purpose.

Do we know where we're going? Are we chasing a paycheck, climbing the corporate ladder without a clear "why," or seeking the world's approval? Or are we living with a sense of direction that not only fits this life but connects us to something far greater?

The Bible speaks directly to this longing. Ephesians 2:10 reminds us, *"For we are God's handiwork, created in Christ Jesus to do good works, which God prepared in advance for us to do."* Mark Twain once said, *"The two most important days in your life are the day you are born and the day you find out why."* Both point to the same truth: You and I were created on purpose, for a purpose.

And while God may not always shout the answer, He often whispers through the things that stir our hearts, spark our energy, and light us up inside. Proverbs 20:5 says, *"The purposes of a person's heart are deep waters, but one who has insight draws them out."* I believe this means that God places something deep within us—and part of our journey is to draw it out with His help.

I hope you don't settle for coasting. I hope you don't let life just happen to you. Start right now. Step boldly into the life God designed specifically for you—a life worthy of your calling, rooted in joy, grounded in prayer, and overflowing with gratitude.

"And we know that in all things
God works for the good of those who love him,
who have been called according to his purpose."
—Romans 8:28

Missing Puzzle Piece

My wife Tracy loves jigsaw puzzles. It's one of her favorite hobbies, something that brings her both focus and joy. She even has a dedicated puzzle table—complete with drawers, shelves, and a puzzle saver, so she can roll it up and take it on the go, if needed. She'll spend hours sorting pieces, assembling the border, and slowly bringing the picture to life one section at a time.

Nothing frustrates her more than getting near the end and realizing... a piece is missing. She'll check under the table, search between the couch cushions, and sometimes even question our Shih Tzu, Zoe (even though in our house, she can do no wrong). Sometimes the piece turns up. Sometimes it doesn't. But just one missing piece can make the whole puzzle feel off.

There was a season in my life when I felt like an incomplete puzzle. It's not that I was unhappy. I had a successful career, a loving family, lifelong friends, money in the bank, and more blessings than I could count. On the outside, everything looked complete. But on the inside, something was off—a quiet, nagging sense that a piece was missing. I couldn't name it, but I could *feel* it. I was restless. I was worn thin. And, over time, I realized the missing piece in my life wasn't about *what* I was doing—but *why*.

I had drifted from my purpose.

Maybe you've felt that too. Many of us go through life with most of the pieces in place: career, family, health, and even faith. But, without purpose, something still feels incomplete. We were created for more than just success—we were created for significance.

Scripture reminds us of this truth: Colossians 1:16 says, *"All things have been created through him and for him."* That longing—that missing piece—is our God-given desire for meaning. Until we connect our lives to His purpose, the picture will always feel unfinished."

When we align our life with God's purpose, everything else starts to make sense. The puzzle comes together. The picture becomes clear. As Frederick Buechner once wrote, "*The place God calls you to is the place where your deep gladness and the world's deep hunger meet.*" With that clarity, we begin to see the unique role our God-given purpose plays in completing the bigger picture of His plan.

"God gives every one of us a unique mission —and He gives us a choice as to whether or not we fulfill that mission."

—Pastor Rick Warren

Don't Use a Hammer

Tracy had her eye on one of those touchless kitchen faucets. The kind where you wave your hand and the water magically turns on like something from The Jetsons cartoon. Naturally, she wanted one for our kitchen.

Now, my dad was the kind of person who could build or fix just about anything. He changed his own oil, wired outlets, and built a two-story storage shed in his backyard—by himself. That Do It Yourself (DIY) gene did not get passed on to me! I proudly claim the ability to change light bulbs, but that's about the extent of my handyman résumé.

Still, I wasn't about to spend $150 on a plumber to install a faucet. How hard could it be? The YouTube video I watched said it would only take 15 minutes. When the old faucet wouldn't slide out easily, I decided to "help" it along… with a hammer. *Just a gentle tap*, I told myself. That tap did the trick—

the faucet came out... and so did a long, visible crack across our Corian countertop.

So instead of saving money, I got to pay a real handyman to replace our countertops—*and* a plumber to replace the faucet—all because I tried to force something. It was a frustrating and expensive lesson. Don't force things! Not faucets. Not circumstances. Not relationships. And certainly not our purpose.

Too often we want instant results, immediate clarity, or instantaneous answers. When life doesn't move according to our timeline, we often reach for a "hammer"—trying to force God's hand, shortcut the process, or manufacture an outcome. But forced purpose never holds; it only leaves cracks behind.

Purpose doesn't work that way. It isn't forced. It takes time, patience, trust, and humility. Sometimes, the best thing we can do is zoom out, look at the bigger picture, and ask for help from a professional. That might mean leaning into wise mentors, trusted friends, or God Himself, in prayer.

When we trust God's timing, we don't just avoid cracks in the countertop—we give our lives the space to take shape exactly as He designed them.

"If you can't figure out your purpose,
figure out your passion.
For your passion will lead you right into your purpose."
—T.D. Jakes

Obsessing Over Sleep

A few years ago, Tracy and I both bought Oura Rings. We wanted to track our sleep, steps, and stress levels. I enjoyed looking at my data daily—it was eye opening. But it also revealed something I wasn't thrilled about: alcohol in the evenings was wrecking my sleep. So much for that beer (or three) before bed.

Every morning, the first thing I did was check my sleep score. I became obsessed with it—so much so that it started hurting my sleep. I later learned there's a name for this: *orthosomnia, a term sleep researchers use to describe anxiety about getting "perfect" sleep that ends up making rest even harder to come by*. I'd go to bed worrying about relaxing enough to sleep. Then I'd wake up in the middle of the night, check the time, and start calculating how many hours I had left to hit my "ideal" score. Ironically, my quest for better rest was sabotaging it.

Eventually, I had to let go. I stopped obsessing over the numbers and focused on rest. That's when my sleep started to improve again.

The same is true with purpose. Sometimes we chase it so anxiously and relentlessly that we miss it. Like sleep, the harder we strain to grab it, the more it slips away. But when we slow down, stop obsessing, and start building a strong foundation, we often begin to see our purpose more clearly.

Psychologists call this ironic process theory—the harder we try not to think about something (like sleep or purpose), the more our brain fixates on it. That's why Scripture points us in a different direction: *"Be still, and know that I am God"* (Psalm 46:10). Sometimes clarity comes not from striving, but from stillness.

It's not always about chasing. Sometimes it's about receiving. Jesus put it this way in Matthew 6:33: *"Seek first his kingdom and his righteousness, and all these things will be given to you as well."*

When we seek Him, our purpose has a way of finding us.

You don't have to force your purpose to appear. Often the most purposeful thing we can do is stop striving, breathe deeply, and create steady habits of faith, prayer, and obedience. With clarity, we'll be ready to step fully into the purpose we were created to live.

"You're never too old to set another goal
or dream another dream."
—C.S. Lewis

Never Too Old

You're never too old to discover your purpose—or to live it out. Colonel Sanders began franchising KFC in his 60s, Ray Kroc started his McDonald's journey at 52, and Michelangelo was still creating masterpieces in his 80s. And Noah? He was over 500 years old when he started building the ark—talk about a late-life adventure.

Everything happens in God's perfect timing—not ours. Ecclesiastes 3:11 reminds us, *"He has made everything beautiful in its time."* Not my time. Not your time. *His* time. The Bible gives us an incredible example of this in the life of Caleb. He was one of the original twelve spies sent by Moses to scout the Promised Land. While ten came back with fear, Caleb and Joshua returned with faith, trusting that God would give them victory. Because of this, they were the only two from their generation allowed to enter the land God had promised.

But here's the part that often gets overlooked: Caleb had to wait 45 years for that promise to come true. During that time, he wandered the desert, watched a whole generation pass away, and waited patiently as the Israelites slowly moved toward the fulfillment of God's word. And then—at 85 years old—Caleb stood before Joshua, the leader of the Israelites, and said: *"I am still as strong today as the day Moses sent me out... Now give me this hill country that the Lord promised me that day."*—Joshua 14:10-12

Caleb didn't ask for an easier path or a quiet retirement. He asked for a mountain. He was still full of vision, still full of faith, and still claiming God's promises. That's what makes Caleb so inspiring: he shows us that our purpose isn't diminished by age and can sharpen with time.

John Bevere, in his book *Extraordinary*, writes: *"There's One Person above all others who desires an extraordinary life for you. He's a Father who delights, like any good father, in the achievements and happiness of His children. His name is God."* Andy Andrews, in *The Noticer*, breaks it down this way: *"God has a purpose for every person. You won't die until that purpose is fulfilled. If you're still alive, you haven't completed what you were put here to do. That means your most important contribution may still be ahead. You still matter—maybe more than ever."*

If we've ever felt like we missed our chance, that our moment has passed—remember Caleb. Remember Colonel Sanders. Remember that if God's not done with us, then we're not done either. The mountain is still ours to climb. Because if we're still breathing, our God-given purpose is still unfolding. That's what this book is about: the foundation of a meaningful, purposeful life—one that's anchored in joy, grounded in prayer, and built on a thankful heart. Jesus said it best in Matthew 7:24: *"Therefore everyone who hears these words of mine and puts them into practice is like a wise man who built his house on the rock."*

We may not know exactly what our "perfect life" looks like, but if we build it on the rock of God's truth—with joy, prayer, and thankfulness—we'll be building something that truly lasts. And sometimes that begins not with lofty ambition but by returning to the basics.

> "Effort and courage are not enough
> without purpose and direction."
> —***John F. Kennedy***

Go West

In 1991, I co-founded my first company, FutureTech Training, with two of my best friends, Russ Peterson Jr. and Clay Lockley. We were in our early 20s, full of energy and ambition, and determined to build something successful. At the time, I thought success itself was my purpose; so I threw myself into work—week after week, year after year—believing that growing our revenues and expanding to new locations was the goal.

A business trip to Singapore changed my perspective in a surprising way. At Changi Airport, I hopped into a taxi, and the driver asked me a simple question: "Where to?"

"West," I said confidently, but jokingly.

He looked at me in the rearview mirror and replied, "Sir, west is a direction—not a destination. If you want to arrive somewhere, you'll need to know exactly where you're going."

That landed like a ton of bricks (and it also confirmed that my humor works about as well in foreign countries as it does in my own).

At that moment, I realized I'd been moving in the general direction of "success" without ever defining what success actually meant for me. Simply saying "I want to be successful" isn't enough. Success without purpose is like heading west without a map—you may be moving, but not necessarily toward what matters.

Living with purpose means moving through life with intention, not just motion. We can work hard, aim high, and still feel lost, if we haven't defined where we truly want to go—and more importantly, why.

Proverbs 16:9 says, *"In their hearts humans plan their course, but the Lord establishes their steps."* Purpose means letting God transform our vague sense of direction into a clear, God-given destination.

So let me ask: are you just "going west?" or are you walking toward a destination God has designed for you? As Andy Stanley puts it, *"Direction, not intention, determines destination."* When we define that destination with Him, we stop wandering and start living with purpose.

"Life is meant to be fun, joyous, and fulfilling.
May each of yours be that.
It's a good life, enjoy it."
—Jim Henson

What is a Meaningful Life?

I've learned a lot about purpose from Arthur Brooks, a social scientist and Harvard professor whose work I follow closely. His book *From Strength to Strength* deeply influenced me, and in one of his *Atlantic* columns, he explains that meaning is built on three pillars:

1. Coherence – the belief that things happen for a reason
2. Purpose – the sense of direction in life
3. Significance – the belief that your life truly matters

When I read this, I paused and thought, *That explains so much about my own journey.* It helped me see how I could have a good job, a full calendar, success by the world's standards, and yet feel restless inside. Without meaning, we can drift. The past can feel confusing, the present can feel unsettled, and when the storms in life hit us, we feel lost at sea.

Arthur writes, *"Without purpose, we can't navigate life's inevitable challenges and crises. When we do have a sense of meaning, we can face life with hope and inner peace."* This rings true—I've experienced it personally. When we live with meaning, we're energized, engaged, and far more resilient.

Here's where it all comes together for me: Arthur's framework aligns perfectly with 1 Thessalonians 5, where Paul urges us to live with joy, to stay in constant prayer, and to give thanks no matter our circumstances. Joy, prayer, and thankfulness aren't just nice ideas—they're the grounding practices that shape a purposeful life. A meaningful life isn't just about achievement; it's about alignment with the One who gives us life.

As Rabbi Harold Kushner wrote: *"Our souls are not hungry for fame, comfort, wealth, or power... our souls are hungry for meaning, for the sense that we have figured out how to live so that our lives matter, so that the world will be at least a little bit different for our having passed through it."*

We weren't created just to pass time or fill space. *We were created on purpose and for a purpose.* When we live that way—rooted in God's love and design for each of us—meaning becomes the center of our days, not just something we chase. And with it comes a peace no hardship can steal. Purpose stops being an abstract idea and becomes the very way we live.

In moments like that, I'm reminded of the song *Walk by Faith* by Jeremy Camp—a quiet reminder that following God often means taking the next step before the whole path is clear.

"Whoever believes in me,
as Scripture has said,
rivers of living water
will flow from within them."
—John 7:38

Be a River, not a Lake

To live with purpose means we keep moving forward. We grow, we stretch, and we allow God to use us as a conduit of His grace, love, and wisdom. In other words: Be a river, not a lake. Rivers are dynamic. They flow, change, and give life to everything around them. Lakes, on the other hand, can become stagnant. They stay where they are, receiving but not releasing. Living with purpose means we don't just collect knowledge, resources, or experiences for ourselves—we let them flow through us, blessing others along the way. As Jesus said in John 7:38, *"Rivers of living water will flow from within them"*—but only if we're willing to move where He sends us.

When you choose to become a river, you must leave the safety of still waters. Leaving your comfort zone is never easy! It means passing through the fear zone, where uncertainty and doubt can creep in. Next, comes the learning zone (I like to call it the sponge zone), where we are filled with wisdom, tools, and perspective. Eventually, we reach the growth zone, where real purpose is found... not in comfort, but in calling.

There's a great example of this in the geography of the Holy Land. The Sea of Galilee is vibrant—full of fish, boats, and life. Why? Because it receives fresh water from the north and then gives it away through the Jordan River in the south. That same river eventually flows into the Dead Sea, a body of water that takes in everything and gives out nothing. Its high salt content makes it impossible for fish to live or plants to grow—*nothing* thrives in it. Even boats can't sail on it. The difference between the two isn't how much they receive, but whether they release.

When we live like a lake—holding tightly to our talents, time, and treasures—without sharing—we stagnate.

In my own life, I've tried to be consistent—sharing my time and talents—whether it's teaching, mentoring, or encouraging others. But I'll admit, I haven't always been as quick to share my treasure. At times, it's been easier to give from my calendar than from my bank account. This is an area where God continues to stretch me to be more like a river and less like a lake.

A purposeful life is not about accumulation—it's about circulation. God doesn't bless us just for our own benefit, but so that we can bless others. Genesis 12:2 says, *"I will bless you, and you will be a blessing to others."*

So ask yourself: Am I storing too much of what God has given me? Will a release make room for more growth and purpose? Because the more we let God's blessings flow through us, the more our lives align with the purpose He created us for.

This week, find one way to "flow" instead of "store"—share your time, share your treasure, or share your talents with someone or someplace (like your favorite non-profit) that would benefit.

"Any structure must have a strong foundation.
The cornerstones anchor the foundation."
—John Wooden

The Sears Tower

Growing up in the Chicago suburbs (I was born in Oak Park, Illinois), I was always fascinated by the Sears Tower (and yes, I still have a hard time calling it the Willis Tower). It stood like a giant among buildings—soaring 1,450 feet above the city, 110 stories—an unmistakable presence in the skyline. When it was completed in 1973, it was the tallest building in the world.

But what's even more impressive than what's visible above ground is what lies beneath.

Before a single steel beam went up, engineers designed a foundation that could handle the building's immense size and weight. Beneath the surface, workers poured enough concrete to build an eight-lane highway stretching five miles long. The tower needed a foundation that would not shift, crack, or crumble under pressure—something unseen—but absolutely essential.

The same is true for us. If we want to live tall and strong—especially when the winds of life start blowing—we need to be grounded. Our foundation is strongest when it is deep and intentional. Jesus made this point in Matthew 7:24–25: *"Everyone who hears these words of mine and puts them into practice is like a wise man who built his house on the rock. The rain came down, the streams rose, and the winds blew and beat against that house; yet it did not fall, because it had its foundation on the rock."*

And the materials that hold us up? Joy, prayer, and thankfulness. They may not look impressive to the world, but they are the concrete foundation for a purposeful life. They may not be flashy, but they sustain us. They allow us to rise. And when we rise on this kind of foundation, we don't just stand tall—we stand secure in the purpose God has designed for us.

"If the foundations are destroyed,
what can the righteous do?"
—Psalm 11:3

This is a Football

My dad always joked that I could weave football into just about any conversation—sometimes it was about the Texas Longhorns—sometimes about one of my fantasy football teams. This story comes from one of the greatest coaches of all time.

At the start of the Green Bay Packers' 1961 training camp—just months after a heartbreaking loss to the Philadelphia Eagles in the NFL Championship Game—legendary coach Vince Lombardi stood before his team holding a familiar object in his hand. "Gentlemen," he said, "this is a football."

He wasn't trying to be funny. Lombardi was reminding his players that greatness begins with mastering the basics. Even among professional athletes at the highest level, he believed the key to success was returning to the foundational truths of the game.

That season, the Packers went on to dominate the league and win the NFL Championship. (It wasn't called the Super Bowl yet—the first one wouldn't take place until 1967.)

In the same way, living with purpose begins with revisiting the basics. Jesus made this clear when asked about the greatest commandment. He boiled all of Scripture down to two basics: *"Love the Lord your God with all your heart and with all your soul and with all your mind,"* and *"Love your neighbor as yourself"* (Matthew 22:37–39). We often over-complicate life, looking for meaning in the extraordinary, when it's the ordinary, foundational truths that give us real direction and strength.

And when we master those basics—joy, prayer, and thankfulness—we're building a life strong enough to carry our God-given purpose all the way to the end zone for a touchdown. Or, as Paul put it in 2 Timothy 4:7, *"I have fought the good fight, I have finished the race, I have kept the faith."*

Purpose isn't about flashy plays; it's about finishing well.

"No discipline seems pleasant at the time, but painful.
Later on, however,
it produces a harvest of righteousness and peace
for those who have been trained by it."
—Hebrews 12:11

Start with the Foundation

Albert Einstein once said, *"If you can't explain it simply, you don't understand it well enough."* I've always admired people who can take something complex and break it down so anyone can understand it. Dave Ramsey does this with money. Before he ever talks about investing, buying a house, or building wealth, he starts with the basics—seven "baby steps" that form a clear foundation for financial freedom:

1. Save $1,000 for a starter emergency fund
2. Pay off all debt (except the house) using the debt snowball
3. Save 3–6 months of expenses in a fully funded emergency fund
4. Invest 15% of household income in retirement
5. Save for your children's college fund
6. Pay off your home early
7. Build wealth and give generously

These steps aren't flashy, and they're not always easy—but they work. Why? Because they're rooted in discipline and built on a solid foundation. That same principle shows up in other areas of life. In the world of CrossFit, there's a training model called the "Fitness Pyramid." It's designed to show how true athletic performance is developed layer by layer, from the inside out:

1. Nutrition (Base)
2. Metabolic Conditioning (Cardio and Endurance)
3. Gymnastics (Body Control and Movement Skills)
4. Weightlifting (Strength and Power)
5. Sport/Skill (Application at the Top)

It's not hard to see why the pyramid starts with nutrition. You can't out-train a bad diet. What you fuel your body with determines how well you perform, recover, and grow. Life works the same way. We often want to skip straight to the "building wealth" or "top performance" stages—accomplishments, influence, legacy—without first building the foundation that sustains those things. Jesus used the same imagery when He warned about building on sand versus building on rock (Matthew 7:24–27). Without a solid base, everything eventually crumbles.

I see joy, prayer, and thankfulness as the cornerstone of a meaningful life. They align everything else—how we show up at work, how we love our family, how we respond to setbacks. And just like Einstein's principle, if we can't explain our life's foundation, simply, we probably don't understand it well enough to live it out. Joy, prayer, and thankfulness may sound simple, but they take daily practice. When they become our base, they hold up everything else—and give our purpose the strength to stand tall.

"There is no greater gift you can give or receive
than to honor your calling.
It is why you were born and
how you become most truly alive."
—Oprah Winfrey

Bamboo Tree

During my many business trips to Singapore, I would often visit the Botanic Gardens—one of my favorite places to walk, to pray, to enjoy nature. This is where I first learned how bamboo trees grow. When a bamboo seed is planted, growth begins—but you might not notice it at first.

In the first year, the plant appears dormant. By year two, it still seems barely alive. Even in year three, there's often little visible change. But beneath the surface, something important is happening. The bamboo is developing an intricate root system—anchoring itself, spreading deep and wide, preparing for what's to come.

Then—when that hidden foundation is secure—the bamboo surprises you. Over a period of 60 days, new shoots emerge and rocket upward. Some species can reach up to 90 feet tall, in a matter of months. That kind of explosive growth doesn't happen without preparation. It happens because the bamboo spent years building strength where no one could see it.

The same is true for us. We may go through seasons where nothing seems to be happening—no promotion, no relationship, no breakthrough, no clarity. But underneath, God may be building something deep and lasting in us.

This has been true in my own career. I started Ballooners in college, which gave me my first taste of entrepreneurship and opened the door to becoming an IBM campus rep. From there, Dell hired me, and that experience eventually led Russ and me to launch a computer training company that grew into FutureTech. Later, we co-founded iSpeak, building it into a multimillion-dollar business. Today, I'm privileged to be self-employed as a keynote speaker, traveling the globe to encourage and empower audiences. Each step may have felt ordinary in the moment, but looking back, I can see how God was quietly growing a root system beneath the surface—preparing me for the growth and purpose He had planned all along.

Joy, prayer, and thankfulness may not produce flashy results right away, but like roots, they grow quietly and steadily—and when they do take hold, growth comes strong, fast, and in the exact direction of the purpose God planted in us long ago.

Galatians 6:9 puts it this way: *"Let us not become weary in doing good, for at the proper time we will reap a harvest if we do not give up."*

So let's be patient in the unseen seasons. Growth often feels slow before it feels significant. But God is always at work beneath the surface, even when progress isn't visible. Trust *His* timing. Trust *His* process. Your season of growth will come.

"God doesn't call the qualified.
He qualifies the called."
—Max Lucado

The Power of *Yes*

Moses didn't start out as the confident leader we picture parting the Red Sea. In fact, when God first called him from the burning bush, Moses was full of hesitation. *"Who am I that I should go to Pharaoh and bring the Israelites out of Egypt?"* (Exodus 3:11). He had a whole list of reasons why he wasn't the right man for the job: *"I'm not eloquent... I'm slow of speech and tongue"* (Exodus 4:10). At one point, he even begged God to send someone else. Moses wrestled with self-doubt and imposter syndrome long before those words existed.

This reminds me of Mother Teresa of Calcutta, who once said: *"I know God will not give me anything I can't handle. I just wish He didn't trust me so much."* That honesty captures what so many of us feel when God calls us to something bigger than ourselves.

But God had a purpose for Moses—and despite all his insecurities, Moses eventually said *yes*. That *yes* changed everything. He confronted Pharaoh with courage, led God's people out of slavery, and guided them through miracles, hardships, and wilderness wanderings. He spoke with God face-to-face, delivered the Ten Commandments, and never stopped pointing his people toward the Promised Land—even though he wouldn't enter it himself. His *yes* didn't just impact that moment in history; it set into motion a story that shaped the identity of God's people and ultimately paved the way for Christ.

I think about that often in my own life. There have been times when I hesitated—when I wondered if I was really ready, really qualified, or really the right person. I remember being invited to deliver my first keynote internationally, and my first thought was, "*Who am I to do that?*" But when I said yes, it opened doors I never could have imagined. Some of the most meaningful chapters of my life began not when I felt ready, but when I felt called—and chose to trust God enough to say *yes*.

Pastor Rick Warren once said, "*The most dangerous prayer you can pray is, 'Use me.'*" Dangerous, because God will take you at your word. He will stretch you, grow you, and lead you into places you never expected—just like He did with Moses. Saying *yes* to God is rarely safe or comfortable. But it is *always* significant. Moses' story reminds us that purpose isn't always easy, and it's rarely convenient. But when God calls, He also equips. You don't have to feel qualified. *You just have to be willing*. God often calls us before we feel prepared—but He never calls us without a plan.

So, let me ask you: is there something God is nudging you toward right now? A conversation, a new opportunity, a way to serve, a step of faith? Don't wait until you feel perfectly ready. Be open. Be available. Take that first step. Because saying *yes* to God's call—and praying that bold prayer, "Use me," will always be the first step toward living your purpose.

"I don't want to get to the end of my life and
find that I lived just the length of it.
I want to have lived the width of it as well."
— ***Diane Ackerman***

Well Done Faithful Servant

"Well done, my good and faithful servant." Those are the words from Matthew 25:23 that every Christ follower longs to hear one day—when we finally stand face to face with our Lord in Heaven.

It's a short sentence, but it carries eternal weight. It's the affirmation that our lives mattered, that we ran the race well, that we didn't waste what we were given.

Author Erma Bombeck once said, "*When I stand before God at the end of my life, I would hope that I would not have a single bit of talent left and could say, 'I used everything you gave me.'*"

That's a beautiful picture of what it means to live with purpose. I hope that I can faithfully say this when my time on earth comes to an end.

So, how are you doing? Are you using your time, talents, and treasure to their full potential? Are you living with intention—or drifting? Are you focused on what truly matters, or distracted by what fades?

Here's the good news: you don't need a big platform or a global audience to hear those words. Faithfulness isn't about fame—it's about stewardship. It's about showing up every day with a surrendered heart and doing the best you can with what God has placed in your hands. A purposeful life isn't measured by what the world applauds, but by how closely we walk with God, how faithfully we love others, and how willing we are to use our gifts for *His* glory.

That perspective always brings to mind the song *Well Done* by Moriah Peters—a quiet reminder that the affirmation we're really longing for comes not from the crowd, but from God.

Keep showing up. Keep planting seeds. Keep living with purpose—even when no one else notices. Because one day, when you hear those words— *"Well done, good and faithful servant"*— you'll know it was all worth it. In that moment, you'll see your purpose was fulfilled exactly as God intended.

"The real joy in life comes from
finding your true purpose and
aligning it with what you do every single day."
—Tony Robbins

Pillars of Purpose

Most of us don't wake up asking, *Why am I here?* But we feel it when something's missing—when success doesn't satisfy, when busyness leaves us empty, or when life starts to feel more like motion than meaning.

Before we can live a life overflowing with joy, prayer, and thankfulness, we must wrestle with the deeper question: *Why are we here?*

Purpose gives shape and direction to a life that is steady, rich, and meaningful. Without it, we drift. With it, we move through life with intention, clarity, and direction.

The Apostle Paul gives us a powerful framework in 1 Thessalonians 5:16–18: *"Be joyful always, pray continually, give thanks in all circumstances, for this is God's will for you in Christ Jesus."*

These aren't just suggestions. They're the pillars of a purposeful life:

- ❧ Joy anchors our hearts in hope, no matter what we're facing.
- ❧ Prayer keeps us connected to God, our source of strength and wisdom.
- ❧ Thankfulness reminds us how blessed we already are—even in seasons of waiting or pain.

Individually, each one strengthens us. But together, they create a foundation strong enough to weather storms, endure setbacks, and sustain us through uncertainty.

When these pillars are in place, purpose doesn't just guide us—it steadies us. It shapes how we show up every day, how we persevere when life gets hard, and how we finish the race set before us. Joy, prayer, and thankfulness aren't just good habits—they're God's design for a life that lasts.

"The purpose of life is to be useful,
to be honorable, to be compassionate—
to have it make some difference
that you have lived and lived well."
– Ralph Waldo Emerson

From Purposeful to Joyful

Purpose isn't just about knowing why you're here—it's about

living it out every single day. And the best way to live with purpose is to root yourself in the three pillars of God's design: joy, prayer, and thankfulness.

These aren't just inspiring ideas or self-help habits. They're how we build a life with deep meaning, steady peace, and lasting impact. Purpose gives you direction, but these three pillars give you the strength to walk it out—especially when life doesn't go as planned.

With purpose now in view, it's time to explore the first pillar: joy. Not the fleeting happiness that shifts with circumstances, but the well-being that flows from knowing and trusting God... even when life is far from perfect. This is where the journey takes root. This is where purpose begins to overflow.

Joyful

ADJECTIVE:
Feeling, expressing,
or causing great pleasure or happiness;
full of joy.

C.S. Lewis

"Joy is the serious business of heaven."

Job 8:21

"He will yet fill your mouth with laughter and
your lips with shouts of joy."

Our Call to be Joyful

In this chapter, we explore what it means to be joyful always (1 Thessalonians 5:16)—because joy is more than a fleeting mood or a brief burst of excitement. Joy is a deep and steady gladness that flows from our relationship with God, not from our circumstances. As Nehemiah 8:10 reminds us, *"The joy of the Lord is your strength."*

If joy is our strength, why does it sometimes feel like it's slipping through our fingers? How do we hold on to joy when a wave of uncertainty crashes into our lives and leaves things messy, stressful, and unclear? How do we tell the difference between the deep, lasting joy from God and the temporary lift of circumstantial happiness?

In the pages ahead, we'll look at how to cultivate a joy that isn't dependent on circumstances but is rooted in God's presence and promises.

"When we are no longer able to change a situation, we are challenged to change ourselves."
—Viktor Frankl

The Price of Positivity

One second it was on my head, the next it was gone—lost in the ocean, forever. My favorite Cubs hat, perfectly broken in, perfectly faded (I've been a diehard Cubs fan my whole life, growing up in Chicago); it was the one I wore when I wanted the Cubs to win.

South Padre Island is our happy place. Tracy has been going every year since she was eight, and now it's our tradition too. Sunshine, sand, the sound of the waves—it's hard to be anything but joyful there. Unless, of course, you lose your favorite hat to the ocean.

I wore it into the water to keep the sun off my head. Rookie mistake. A big wave came in, and just like that, my hat was gone.

I searched frantically in the surf. Then I paced the shoreline, hoping it would wash up. No luck. By the time I made my way back to our spot on the beach, my frustration had turned into anger. Before I did or said something I would later regret, I announced I was going back to the condo to have a pity party.

Hours later, Tracy came back smiling. "Good news!" she said. I thought she'd found my hat. Instead, she'd found the exact same one online for $25; it would be delivered to our condo the next day.

I laughed—then cringed. I'd wasted an entire afternoon in one of my favorite places, with my favorite people, sulking over something that could easily be replaced for less than the cost of dinner.

Right then I realized I had a "price" for my positivity... and it was embarrassingly low. How often do we do this in life? We can waste minutes frustrated over traffic, hours irritated by delays, days stewing over small slights, or years nursing grudges. Now, when frustration creeps in, I ask myself one simple question: "Is this worth the price of my joy?"

Every morning, God deposits 86,400 seconds into your life account. You can spend them however you choose—but at midnight, whatever you haven't used is gone forever. No roll-overs. No saving it for later. The next morning, the account is refilled, but yesterday's balance is gone.

Time is God's gift to us, and how we spend that time reveals what we truly value. Why spend what we can never get back on something that doesn't matter?

Philippians 4:4 says, *"Rejoice in the Lord always. I will say it again: Rejoice!"* And Proverbs 19:11 reminds us, *"Good sense makes one slow to anger, and it is his glory to overlook an offense."* Sometimes, overlooking the offense—or the inconvenience (or the lost hat)—is the best investment we can make in our joy.

Jesus tells us in John 10:10, *"The thief comes only to steal and kill and destroy; I have come that they may have life, and have it to the full."* Our enemy would love to steal our joy with small frustrations, but Jesus came so that we could experience abundant life—joy that isn't for sale at a cheap price.

Joy can be stolen in an instant, if we let it—but it can also be guarded and grown. The rest of this chapter is about discovering the kind of joy that not only weathers life's storms but also brings a smile to the heart of God—joy that reflects His desire for us to experience a taste of heaven here on earth. Along the way, we'll explore simple, powerful habits—like showing kindness, knowing your core values, and taking a mindful walk—which can weave joy into the fabric of your everyday life.

Our joy is too valuable to give away freely to frustration. We must decide ahead of time what's worth our peace—and make that price so high that small annoyances can't afford it. Think of the last time you let something steal your joy. Was it worth the cost? This week, when frustration comes knocking, pause and ask yourself: "Is this worth the price of my positivity?"

"Most of your life will not be extraordinary.
Most of your life will be simple things,
done regularly.
If you are only going to be happy when you're on vacation,
after a lush payday, after a big career win,
you're going to spend most of your life really dissatisfied.
You either learn to love the day as it is,
or you don't learn to love life at all."
-Brianna Wiest

Feel All the Feels

Tracy and I recently re-watched *Inside Out 2* (highly recommend). It reminded me of something I often teach: we can't, and shouldn't, be positive all the time. Frustration, anger, grief—these are part of being human. Happiness requires unhappiness; without contrast, joy wouldn't mean as much.

Ecclesiastes 3:4 reminds us there is *"a time to weep and a time to laugh, a time to mourn and a time to dance."* God never intended us to live in only one emotional lane.

When my mom passed away last year, I grieved. When the Longhorns lost in the college football playoffs, I was upset. When I had to get both hips replaced because of the medication I take to prevent my kidney from rejecting, I was angry. These moments hurt—some in small ways, others in life-altering ways—and pretending otherwise would have been dishonest and more harmful than feeling the feelings.

The trouble comes when we believe we must be positive no matter what. That's called *toxic positivity*—the idea that we should maintain a cheerful mindset in the middle of loss, hardship, or crisis. It pressures us to hide our pain, instead of working through it, to put on a smile, instead of processing the harder emotions. Real joy isn't about plastering a grin over grief or frustration; it's about giving yourself permission to feel the full range of emotions—trusting that joy will return in its time.

Annie McKee puts it simply: *"I learned you need to take care of your emotional life, just as you do your physical health."*

True emotional health means acknowledging what we feel without judgment. Research from the University of California shows that people who suppress emotions experience higher levels of stress and weakened immune responses. Accepting, rather than suppressing emotions, reduces stress, lowers anxiety and depression, and improves overall well-being. This authenticity builds self-awareness, resilience, and a deeper capacity to navigate life's ups and downs.

The danger isn't in feeling hard emotions—it's in getting stuck there. Edwin Louis Cole put it this way: *"You don't drown by falling in the water; you drown by staying there."* Psalm 34:18 echoes this truth: *"The Lord is close to the brokenhearted and saves those who are crushed in spirit."* We've all faced setbacks, but the key is not to set up camp in that place.

One way I help people avoid getting stuck is by teaching them to spot the ANTs—*Automatic Negative Thoughts*—thoughts that creep in if we're not careful. Psychologist Susan David calls this *emotional agility*: the ability to be present with your emotions without getting hooked by them. It starts with noticing what's happening, naming the feeling, and then choosing your response, instead of reacting impulsively. Lou Holtz puts it simply: *"Life is 10% what happens to you and 90% how you respond to it."* In my *Positivity Under Pressure* keynote, I compare this to being a thermostat rather than a thermometer—a thermostat reads the environment and responds with intentional adjustments, influencing the climate, instead of just mirroring it.

I choose to experience the full range of human emotions—joy, sadness, anger, fear, surprise, disgust, even contempt—the very emotions Dr. Paul Ekman identified as universal across cultures. God designed us to feel deeply; each emotion is a signal, telling us something about our inner world and our circumstances. When we embrace our feelings, we can process, learn, and grow. When we suppress them, they don't disappear—they often fester, leading to stress, anxiety, and eventually burnout.

The goal isn't to pretend everything is fine; it's to face reality with optimism. Jesus Himself modeled this. He wept at Lazarus' tomb (John 11:35)—showing us that grief and faith can coexist. Positivity should never come at the expense of authenticity. When we give ourselves permission to feel, and then choose how to respond, we find a healthier, more grounded sense of joy.

When you allow yourself to feel a full range of emotions, you're living as God designed you. The difference between staying stuck and moving forward is what you choose to do after the feeling comes. Don't drown in the water, swim toward the shore. Let joy be your compass, even in rough seas.

This week, when frustration, sadness, or fear shows up, pause and name it. Ask God what He wants to show you, through it, and then take one small step forward. Your emotions don't have to control you—but they can guide you, grow you, and point you back to the One who gave them to you in the first place.

"I have learned to be content
whatever the circumstances."
—Philippians 4:11

Control the Controllables

When I first read Stephen Covey's *The 7 Habits of Highly Effective People*, one concept jumped out and has stuck with me—the Circle of Concern. Later, in *The 7 Habits of Highly Effective Teens*, his son Sean Covey simplified it into two clear categories: Things Outside My Control (the outer circle) and Things I Control (the inner circle). The inner circle is where our actions and choices make a difference. The outer circle includes things you simply can't change: the weather, the economy, the stock market, the past, and other people's choices and opinions. The inner circle covers what you can change: our thoughts, our words, our actions, our attitude, our effort, and our boundaries.

I had a vivid reminder of this at a pickleball tournament in Galveston, a few years ago. The wind was brutal—strong enough to push the ball halfway across the court—before it landed. Players were groaning and blaming the conditions. For the first few points, I caught myself getting frustrated, too. But I remembered the Circle of Control. I couldn't stop the wind, but I could control how I responded. I adjusted my game, focused harder, and treated the wind as a creative challenge. My mood lifted, my game improved—and we ended up taking second place. Life will always have its "wind" moments—circumstances we can't change. It might be a difficult coworker, a delayed flight, an unexpected change in plans, or a literal gust messing with your serve. We can't control such things—but we can control how we show up in the middle of them. The Bible gives us the same wisdom: *"Do not worry about tomorrow, for tomorrow will worry about itself"* (Matthew 6:34), and *"Fix your thoughts on what is true, noble, right, pure, lovely, and admirable"* (Philippians 4:8). Both remind us to focus on what we can choose today—to do our best and trust God with the rest.

Decades of research, beginning with psychologist Julian Rotter's work on "locus of control," show that when we focus our energy on what we can influence—our thoughts, choices, and actions—we experience less stress and build greater resilience than when we dwell on things outside our control.

Anxiety grows when we live in the outer circle, obsessing over what we can't change. Peace grows when we live in the inner circle, doing what we can and releasing the rest. There's an old proverb that says, *"You can't control the wind, but you can adjust your sails."* This quote offers a powerful image: though we can't change our circumstances, we can choose how to respond—and in doing so, steer the course of our lives.

Every day, we decide where to spend our mental and emotional energy. Let's spend it on what we can truly influence, allowing God to handle what's beyond our reach. Life feels so much lighter when we stop carrying what was never ours to hold in the first place.

This week, when frustration rises, pause and ask: "Is this in my control or out of my control?" If it's outer-circle stuff, practice acceptance. If it's inner-circle stuff, take action. We can't control everything—but we can always control how we show up. And sometimes, that's all it takes to change everything.

"Your kingdom come,
your will be done,
on earth as it is in heaven."
—Matthew 6:10

Beyond the Gates and Tunnels

Many years back, we took a family vacation to Disney World. We stayed at the Wilderness Lodge; a beautiful property tucked among tall pines, with a grand stone fireplace in the lobby. It felt like a national park resort, but with a touch of Disney magic. One of the highlights was the water taxi ride to the Magic Kingdom. Kip and Kait were ecstatic. They'd spent the morning exploring the lodge, swimming in the pool, and now we were on a boat gliding across the Seven Seas Lagoon toward the most magical place on earth. As we docked, we could feel the excitement rising.

When we stepped off the boat, we were greeted by the beautiful and iconic floral Mickey Mouse display—bright red, golden yellow, and deep black blooms. Behind it were two brick tunnels leading under the train station, with one of the Magic Kingdom steam engines chugging above. The air itself felt different—filled with music, laughter, and the buttery smell of popcorn—there was truly magic in the air. Photographers were waiting, ready to take our family picture (smiling in our matching Disney shirts) in front of the flowers.

And then—imagine this—we got right back on the water taxi and went back to the lodge. Of course, we didn't actually do that. But, if we had, we would have missed something far greater just through those tunnels: Main Street U.S.A.,

Cinderella's Castle, Mickey Mouse, the parades, the rides, the fireworks... all the wonder that makes Disney, Disney. The entrance was good. But the magic inside was great. Jim Collins wrote, *"Good is the enemy of great."* I think that's how God sees many of us living our lives—content to stand at the gate, enjoying the view—but never stepping fully into the abundant life He's prepared for us.

Jesus said in John 10:10, *"I have come that they may have life, and have it to the full."* That's not a life of just enough—that's a life overflowing with purpose, joy, and peace. Ephesians 3:20 reminds us that God is able to do "immeasurably more than all we ask or imagine, according to his power that is at work within us." Sometimes, stepping into that life requires letting go of comfort, familiarity, and even what we perceive to be good things, so we can walk into the great things that God has planned for us.

This week, take one small step toward something that feels "just beyond the gate" in your life. Maybe it's trying a new activity, having a deeper conversation with someone you love, starting or stopping a habit you've been putting off, or saying yes to a God-prompted opportunity that feels a little scary.

Our Heavenly Father isn't just offering us survival–He is offering us a life so rich it feels like heaven on earth. Don't settle for a picture at the entrance, when you've been invited into the whole park.

When you think about your life right now, are you still waiting for the "perfect" time to start? Are you standing at the gate, or walking inside? What "tunnels" might God be asking you to walk through in faith, trusting that something greater is waiting for you just beyond? Joy isn't found in standing at the gate, but in stepping into the fullness of God's presence and promises.

"Sometimes your joy is the source of your smile,
but sometimes your smile can be the source of your joy."
—Thich Nhat Hanh

Brighten a Room

We've all met someone who can brighten a room... by leaving it. I use that line in my keynote presentations as a joke, but there's a lot of truth behind it—emotions really are contagious. The way we carry ourselves doesn't just affect us; it ripples out to everyone around us.

Researchers Nicholas Christakis of Yale and James Fowler of the University of California, San Diego, studied how moods spread through social networks and found striking results: your emotional state can influence your spouse by 8%, your next-door neighbor by 34%, and your coworkers by 20%. In other words, the way we show up matters—not just for us, but for others, every single day.

Psychologists call this *emotional contagion*—the tendency for people to "catch" the emotions of those around them. You've probably felt it: when someone walks in with genuine joy, the whole atmosphere suddenly feels lighter. On the flip side, when someone enters with negativity, it can feel like a dark cloud rolls in.

Jim Rohn famously said, *"We are the average of the five people we spend the most time with."* That idea stuck with me because it made me think about my inner circle—the people whose influence shapes how I think, act, and grow. Then my friend Russ Peterson Jr. added a perspective that made me pause. He said, *"We're not just shaped by others; we're shaping them too."*

That's powerful. Every day, through our attitude, words, and presence, we're becoming part of someone else's 'average.' Our friends, coworkers, spouse, and children are all being shaped, in part, by the way we choose to show up.

This is why cultivating joy isn't just about feeling good; it's about how we influence others. Whether we realize it or not, we are a thermostat in every room we enter—setting the emotional temperature. As Maya Angelou once said, *"People will forget what you said, people will forget what you did, but people will never forget how you made them feel."*

That idea always brings to mind the song *Difference Maker* by Needtobreathe—a reminder that joy isn't just something we feel, it's something we carry into every room we enter.

Our presence has lasting impact. Proverbs 15:13 says, *"A glad heart makes a cheerful face, but by sorrow of heart the spirit is crushed."* When our hearts are filled with joy, it shows—not in a forced smile, but in a genuine warmth that others can feel. Proverbs 17:22 adds, *"A cheerful heart is good medicine, but a crushed spirit dries up the bones."*

Joy doesn't just lift others; it restores and strengthens us too. Our presence changes the atmosphere. As Jon Gordon often writes, we can either be energy givers or energy drainers. Let's choose to walk into every room as bringers of light, not energy vampires. When people think about how they feel after being with us, what do we want them to say?

Think about the last three rooms you entered—your home, your office, or a social gathering. What emotional temperature did you set?

This week, make it your goal to walk into every room as someone whose presence lifts the atmosphere and leaves people better than you found them.

\|/

"Don't chase momentary happiness
at the expense of lasting joy.
Invest in the kind of joy
that doesn't disappear when the moment ends."
—Kevin Karschnik

Time in the Market

I mentioned earlier that my son Kip is a Certified Financial Planner. One of his favorite sayings is: *"It's not about timing the market—it's about time in the market."* In other words, don't try to guess the perfect moment to invest—stay invested for the long haul.

It's tempting to chase the quick win. In money terms, that's like trying to "time the market"—buying and selling at just the right moment to maximize gains. Sometimes it works, but more often it leads to frustration and missed opportunities. Kip coaches his clients to think bigger, to focus on the long-term goal, ride out the ups and downs, and trust that steady, consistent investing will pay off.

The same principle applies to our joy. We can live for short bursts of happiness—a new purchase, a vacation, a "perfect" moment—but that's hedonic happiness: a pleasure that fades as quickly as it comes. It's the emotional equivalent of a short-term trade.

True, lasting joy is more like eudaimonic happiness—the fulfillment that comes from living with meaning, purpose, and alignment with God's plan. That kind of joy isn't dependent on circumstances. It grows over time, rooted in prayer, gratitude, and trust in God's faithfulness.

Psychologist Martin Seligman, known as the father of positive psychology, describes this deeper well-being through the PERMA model: Positive emotion, Engagement, Relationships, Meaning, and Accomplishment. Real joy is not just about feeling good, but about being engaged in life, cultivating healthy relationships, living with purpose, and celebrating progress toward what matters most.

Galatians 6:9 reminds us: *"Let us not become weary in doing good, for at the proper time we will reap a harvest if we do not give up."* In other words, stay invested. Keep showing up. Your joy will grow if you give it time.

When we focus on the long game—in our finances, in our relationships, in our faith—we build something far stronger than fleeting happiness. We build a foundation that can weather the storms. Don't chase momentary happiness at the expense of lasting joy. Joy compounds when we stay invested in what matters most, even when results aren't immediate.

Where in your life have you been chasing quick wins instead of staying committed for the long haul? How can you "stay invested" this week in your faith, relationships, or personal growth so your joy continues to grow over time?

"Wearing a linen ephod,
David was dancing before the Lord with all his might."
—2 Samuel 6:14

Dance Before the Lord

David's life was a mix of triumphs and trials: shepherd, warrior, fugitive, king. Yet through it all, one thing never changed: his deep, unshakable joy in the Lord. That joy showed up in his psalms, in his prayers, and sometimes, in his dancing. One of the most memorable moments came when David brought the Ark of the Covenant back to Jerusalem (2 Samuel 6). This wasn't just a sacred artifact—the Ark represented the very presence of God with His people. For years, it had been away from the city. Now, it was finally coming home. The streets were alive with celebration. Musicians played harps, tambourines, and trumpets. Crowds lined the road. And there, in the middle of it all, was King David—not sitting on a royal chariot but leaping and twirling with "all his might" before the Lord. His joy was so overflowing that he didn't care how it looked to anyone else.

David wasn't dancing for applause. He wasn't performing for the crowd. He was worshiping—body, mind, and spirit—because the presence of God was worth celebrating with everything he had. Psalm 16:11 captures the heartbeat behind his dance: "*You make known to me the path of life; in your presence there is fullness of joy; at your right hand are pleasures forevermore.*" Psalm 150 echoes the same call: "*Let everything that has breath praise the Lord.*"

When was the last time we let ourselves feel that unrestrained joy in God's presence? Not a polite smile, not a nod during a hymn—but joy that bubbles over and refuses to be contained? That's the kind of joy David knew. C.S. Lewis once said, "*Joy is the serious business of heaven.*" If that's true, then worship is our joyful rehearsal.

The joy God offers isn't reserved for special events or perfect circumstances. It's available every day—in a sunrise, answered prayer, and the quiet assurance that He is with us. Maybe our version of dancing before the Lord is singing loudly in church even if we're off-key, laughing freely with our family, or simply expressing gratitude out loud in the middle of the day.

If we've been holding back our worship, afraid of what others might think, let's remember David. One Sunday in church, I thought about this myself. I've never been shy about yelling *"Texas Fight!"* at the top of my lungs in Darrell K Royal–Texas Memorial Stadium with 100,000 fans all around me. Yet for years, I hesitated to sing out loud in church because I didn't think my voice was good enough. Somewhere along the way, I realized how backwards that was. If I can shout without restraint for my Texas Longhorns, why wouldn't I sing out with joy for the God who gave me life? Our joy might not look like David's dance, but the heart behind it can be the same—unashamed, unfiltered worship.

This week let's find one way to express joy without holding back. Dance, sing, laugh, or praise with abandon, knowing our audience is God alone. Joy isn't meant to be bottled up—it's meant to be lived out loud for the One who gave it to us.

"You can't start the next chapter of your life if you keep re-reading the last one."

—Michael McMillan

Let Go of the Banana

There's a simple and well-known way to catch a monkey in South Africa. Hunters place a banana inside a wooden trap with a hole just big enough for the monkey's hand to fit through. The monkey reaches in, grabs the banana, and with its fist tightly holding the prize, it can't fit back through the hole. The monkey could be free in an instant... all it has to do is let go of the banana. But it won't. It holds on, even as hunters approach. What feels like a prize is actually a prison.

I've had my own "banana moments". Times when I've held on to something far too long—a friendship that had become unhealthy, a stock I thought would bounce back, a project I didn't have the bandwidth for, even stuff I've accumulated and, instead of donating it, I put it in a closet, or the attic. In each case, I told myself I couldn't let go—that it was too important, too valuable, too much a part of me. But the truth was, it wasn't adding joy to my life anymore; it wasn't a treasure, it was a weight. I think we've all been there—clinging to *something* that feels safe, that we think we need, while it is secretly keeping us stuck.

Corrie ten Boom once said, *"You must hold everything in your hands lightly, because the Father will take it away from you."* That's a tough lesson, but a freeing one. When we hold on too tightly, we can miss what God is trying to give us instead.

Jesus spoke about this kind of letting go in Matthew 6:19–21: *"Do not store up for yourselves treasures on earth... but store up for yourselves treasures in heaven... For where your treasure is, there your heart will be also."* Wow, have I struggled with that concept my whole life. Sometimes, the "banana" we're holding onto is a possession, sometimes it's a relationship, and sometimes it's simply an old way of thinking. But if it's keeping us from the life God is calling us to live, it's time to let go.

Hebrews 12:1 gives us the same picture: *"Let us throw off everything that hinders and the sin that so easily entangles, and let us run with perseverance the race marked out for us."* Letting go doesn't mean giving up or quitting. It means making space—space for peace, space for joy, space for God to put something better in our hands. An open hand is the posture of both surrender and receiving.

The very thing we're clinging to might be the thing keeping us stuck. Sometimes, the bravest thing we can do is to let go and trust that God has something better waiting for us on the other side of surrender.

So what "banana" are you holding onto right now? What good might happen if you let go and trust God? How can this simple act open the door for more freedom and joy in your life?

"We should make the most of what God gives,
both the bounty and the capacity to enjoy it,
accepting what's given and delighting in the work.
It's God's gift!
God deals out joy in the present, the now."
—Ecclesiastes 5:20 (Message Bible)

The Rhythm of Joy

For me, life is all about balance—the yin and the yang. In Chinese philosophy, the yin represents stillness and rest. The yang represents movement and energy. They aren't opposites that fight—they are complementary forces that complete each other. Each needs the other to be complete.

When I walked five hundred miles on the French Route of the Camino de Santiago in June of 2025, I felt this truth in a new way. The physical challenge of the journey (yang) was balanced by the quiet reflection of the long hours alone with my thoughts (yin). The conversations with fellow pilgrims were balanced by the silent stretches where all I heard was the crunch of my shoes on the trail. There was movement and stillness, challenge and peace, people and solitude—and each gave the other meaning.

Back home, it was easy to lose that balance. My default setting always leans toward yang—go, achieve, accomplish, push forward (I'm a 3 after taking the Enneagram assessment.) But life isn't meant to be lived in constant motion. On the other hand, it's not meant to be pure yin either—sitting still, meditating, and avoiding challenges. We flourish when we live in the rhythm between the two. Romans 12:16–18 encourages us to *"live in harmony with one another"* and to *"do all that you can to live in peace with everyone."* That kind of peace isn't just about avoiding conflict—it's about finding the right rhythm in life: a time to work and a time to rest, a time to strive and a time to be still, a time to pour out and a time to be filled.

The yin-yang symbol also carries a deeper reminder: even in difficult seasons, we shouldn't resist moments of joy. And, in good seasons, we can't ignore that hardship will eventually come. The ability to embrace both—to welcome joy in struggle and stay grounded in abundance—creates a deeper, steadier kind of happiness. It's not about living only in one state or the other, but accepting that both are a part of the fabric of life. Real joy comes when we find the flow between them—like the tide rolling in and out, or a song that alternates between soft and loud. Without stillness, movement burns us out. Without movement, stillness stagnates us. Together, they create a full, vibrant life.

This week, look at your own rhythms. Are you leaning too far into action and achievement? Or too far into rest and retreat? Take one small step toward the middle—pause for a moment of stillness before diving into a busy day, or add a burst of movement to re-energize a slow one.

God designed life with seasons, cycles, and rhythms for a reason. The yin and yang of our days are both gifts. When we learn to flow between them—to move and to rest, to strive and to pause—we discover a steadier, deeper joy. That joy exists in the balance, where movement and stillness meet, and where God invites us to walk with Him.

"It's not hard to make decisions
when you know what your values are."
—Roy Disney

Live Your Values

I believe the foundation of lasting joy is knowing your values—what matters most to you—and then aligning your life so your choices reflect them. When life is out of sync with your values, it creates friction; when it's aligned, it creates peace, clarity, and joy.

Brené Brown puts it this way: *"Living into our values means that we do more than profess our values, we practice them."* I've noticed it in my life—when my thoughts, words, and actions all point in the same direction as my core values, life just feels right. But here's the catch—you can't live by your values if you don't know what they are.

If you've never clarified your core values, here's a simple way to start:

1. Make a list of what matters most. Write down moments in your life when you've felt proud, fulfilled, or deeply at peace. What qualities or priorities were present?

2. Narrow it down. Identify three values that show up again and again — things like faith, family, adventure, generosity, learning, creativity, integrity, or health.
3. Write a Core Value Statement. This is a simple sentence that reminds you who you are and how you want to show up in the world.

Here are mine:

- What Matters Most to me: God, Tracy, Kip, Kait, Positivity, Success, Impact, Humor.
- My Core Values: Faith, Family, Optimism.
- My Core Value Statement: I am faith and family driven, and I lead with optimism to achieve success.

Two years ago, Tracy and I were on vacation in South Padre Island—one of our favorite places to relax and recharge. I got an offer for a speaking engagement in Boston. It was a great opportunity, but it meant I'd have to miss two days of our trip. I said yes. Tracy wasn't upset, but I felt tension in my body—something was off. My choice put work above my marriage—the very opposite of what I had declared in my core values. It wasn't that the work was wrong, but in that moment, it wasn't right for my priorities. That experience reminded me that living your values isn't about big declarations—it's about the small, everyday decisions that either honor them or chip away at them.

When we have clarity, decision-making gets easier. We start asking, "Does this choice reflect my values?" If it doesn't, we can adjust. If it does, we can move forward with confidence.

The Bible affirms the power of living with this kind of integrity. Proverbs 4:25–27 says: *"Let your eyes look straight ahead; fix your gaze directly before you... do not swerve to the right or the left; keep your foot from evil."*

When our eyes are fixed on what matters most, we avoid distractions that pull us off course. Psalm 139:23–24 offers a powerful prayer for alignment: *"Search me, God, and know my heart; test me and know my anxious thoughts. See if there is any offensive way in me, and lead me in the way everlasting."*

One of the biggest joy-drains in life is trying to live by someone else's values. Steve Jobs once said, *"Your time is limited, so don't waste it living someone else's life."* When we compare our lives to others, we can start chasing what matters to them, instead of what God has uniquely placed in our hearts. Our values are a part of our God-given design—embracing them leads to peace, confidence, and joy.

Joy comes from living in alignment with our deepest values, not from chasing what impresses others. Clarity creates confidence, and confidence creates peace.

Have you clearly identified your core values? If not, set aside time this week to write them down and create your own Core Value Statement. If you already know what your core values are, where in your life are you most aligned—and where might you need to make a change?

"Whoever pursues righteousness and love
finds life, prosperity, and honor."
—Proverbs 21:21

The Wheel of Life

Knowing and living our core values is essential. Once we're clear on what matters most to us, the next question is: How well is our life aligned with those values?

That's where the Wheel of Life comes in. It's a simple but powerful tool that helps us see where life feels balanced—and where it might be a little wobbly. The goal isn't perfection, but awareness—so we can make small, intentional changes that bring us more balance and joy.

This idea fits perfectly with *The Rhythm of Joy*—life works best when there's harmony between movement and stillness, challenge and rest, people and solitude. The Wheel of Life gives us a way to see where that harmony is thriving and where it might be out of sync.

The Wheel of Life was first created in the 1960s by Paul J. Meyer, founder of the Success Motivation Institute. Since then, many coaches and leaders have adapted it, but the basic concept has stayed the same. Here's how to use it:

1. Draw a circle and divide it into 8–10 wedges, like slices of a pie.
2. Label each wedge with a different key area of life. Here are some examples to get you started:
   - Health & Fitness – Your physical well-being, energy, and daily habits.
   - Work & Career – Your job, business, or primary daily work.
   - Hobbies & Fun – Activities and interests you do just for enjoyment.
   - Emotional Well-being – Your mood, mindset, mental health, and resilience.
   - Finances – How confident and at peace you feel about money.
   - Faith & Spiritual Growth – Your connection to God and spiritual practices.
   - Family & Relationships – Spouse, kids, extended family.

- Friends & Community – Social connections and support network.
- Learning & Growth – Curiosity, education, and skill development.

3. For each area, rate your current level of satisfaction on a scale from 1 (very dissatisfied) to 10 (completely satisfied).

Mark those scores on the wheel, then connect the dots. This gives a snapshot of where we're investing our time and energy in this season of life. If the shape looks jagged or uneven, the "ride" will feel bumpy—that's a visual clue about where to focus attention.

When I first did this exercise years ago, I noticed my work and financial "spokes" were strong, but hobbies, exercise, and healthy eating were almost nonexistent. That awareness prompted small but meaningful changes —like playing pickleball with Tracy, and making better food choices. The point isn't to hit all 10s (that's not realistic), but to create awareness so we can intentionally invest our limited time and energy where it matters most.

Proverbs 4:26 urges us to *"give careful thought to the paths for your feet and be steadfast in all your ways,"* and Philippians 4:5 reminds us to *"let your gentleness be evident to all. The Lord is near."* Together, these verses remind us to walk with both intention and grace—toward others and toward ourselves.

The Wheel of Life gives us a clear snapshot of where we may be drifting off course and invites us to gently redirect. When life feels out of alignment, it's not a failure—it's an opportunity to pause, make small adjustments, and step forward with renewed purpose.

This week, draw your own Wheel of Life. Look for the

areas that are strong and the ones that need more attention. Then choose one small action to strengthen a weaker area. Over time, those little adjustments can help us live more fully in the rhythm of joy.

"When you arise in the morning,
think of what a precious privilege it is to be alive,
to breathe, to think, to enjoy, to love."
– Marcus Aurelius

Joy Starts Here

How you start your day sets the tone for the rest of it. The Bible reminds us in Psalm 118:24, *"This is the day that the Lord has made; let us rejoice and be glad in it."* Each sunrise is an invitation to choose joy.

After identifying my core values and using the Wheel of Life to see where I was out of balance, I knew I had to create a daily rhythm that would help me live more intentionally.

For me, that rhythm starts every morning with a set of habits I call **JAMSSS**—Journal, Aim, Mindfulness, Stretch, Sunshine, and Smile.

This routine was born out of a hard lesson. On July 23, 2001, Dr. Robert O. Morgan told me it was time for a kidney transplant. Having been diagnosed with IGA Nephropathy back in 1991, I knew this day would eventually come. He explained the surgery and recovery plan, then said something unexpected: *"Your attitude will play an important role in how well you recover."*

I've never forgotten his words. I couldn't control the surgery or the lab results—but I could control my mindset—control the controllables. So I became a student of joy. I read books, listened to experts, and tested practices in my life. What I discovered confirmed what psychologist Dr. Sonja Lyubomirsky, professor of psychology at UC Riverside and author of one of my favorite books *The How of Happiness*, has shown in her research: up to 40% of our long-term happiness comes from the intentional activities we choose every day. In other words, joy is not just something you feel—it's something you do.

One of the best times to do this is first thing in the morning. Studies show that 80% of Americans check their phones within 10 minutes of waking up (globally, it's 71%). Doing this disrupts your brain from its natural, restorative alpha and theta wave states into high-alert beta waves—the stress zone—before you've even had coffee. Instead, give yourself the gift of a gentle, grounded start.

Here's how I use **JAMSSS** to set the tone for my day:

J — Journal

Writing down your thoughts and emotions is like clearing the mental windshield before you hit the road each day. Habakkuk 2:2 tells us to *"write the vision; make it plain on tablets, so he may run who reads it."* This process helps us process what's on our mind, see patterns we might otherwise miss, and approach the day with clarity.

Psychologists have found that expressive writing can improve emotional regulation, reduce stress, and boost overall well-being. Think of it as a daily mental declutter—clearing out yesterday's noise—so we can focus on today's possibilities.

Why It Works: Journaling slows you down long enough to provide clarity with our words, and that process alone changes how your brain processes them. Dr. James Pennebaker, a pioneer in expressive writing research, has shown that writing about your thoughts and feelings improves mental clarity, strengthens your immune system, and even lowers blood pressure.

And while these prompts aren't *only* about gratitude, studies from Dr. Robert Emmons (UC Davis) and Dr. Michael McCullough (University of Miami) found that people who kept short daily or weekly written reflections—especially those that included what they appreciated—experienced better sleep, increased optimism, and made greater progress toward personal goals. The bottom line: putting pen to paper primes your mind for focus, optimism, and purposeful action.

How I Use It: Each morning I answer three simple prompts:

- *I am looking forward to...* This gets me thinking about something positive on the horizon, no matter how small.
- *I am grateful for...* This shifts my perspective toward appreciation (we'll explore this more deeply in the Thankful chapter).
- *I will let go of...* This helps me release anything that could weigh me down, whether it's a worry, resentment, or self-criticism.

My Action Plan (MAP): Spend 3-minutes each morning with these prompts. Don't overthink it—just write whatever comes to mind. This isn't about perfect sentences, spelling, or grammar; it's about clearing space for joy.

A — Aim

Most people ease into their day reacting to whatever shows up first—an email, a text, a social media post, or the news. The problem? When you start in reaction mode, you've already handed over control of your focus.

Setting an aim is like Proverbs 21:5 in action: *"The plans of the diligent lead surely to abundance."* Setting a daily aim is like deciding on a destination before you start the car—you still might take a few scenic detours, but you know where you're headed.

Why It Works: Research from Harvard Business School on what's called the *Progress Principle* shows that nothing fuels motivation and well-being more than making small, meaningful progress in work that matters. Setting a daily aim creates exactly that—it gives you a clear way to notice forward movement, even on hard days.

Studies published in *Frontiers in Psychology* show that intention-setting increases follow-through by priming the brain's prefrontal cortex to recognize and act on opportunities. Visualization activates many of the same neural pathways as actual performance, which boosts confidence and makes it more likely you'll live out your aims. And when your intentions are tied to your core values, they strengthen your sense of purpose—a key ingredient for resilience and joy.

How I Use It: Each morning, before I open my laptop or check my phone, I set one to three clear intentions for the day. Sometimes these are tasks and sometimes they are values-driven actions that guide how I want to show up. They might sound like:

- Today, I will be kind to myself.
- Today, I will encourage someone with a phone call or a text.

❧ Today, I will be fully engaged in our team meeting.

Martha Beck, in *Finding Your Own North Star*, suggests visualizing your perfect day… imagining in detail what you'll do, how you want to feel, and how you'll interact with others. This helps you not just hope for a great day but design it. I mentally walk through the day ahead, picturing myself navigating conversations and meetings with a positive mindset.

<u>My Action Plan (MAP):</u> Before diving into the noise of the day, take a few quiet minutes to write down one to three intentions in a journal or notebook. Keep them short, specific, and rooted in your values. Then close your eyes and visualize yourself carrying them out—see where you'll be, imagine the people you'll interact with, and feel the emotions you want to bring into those moments. This short ritual shifts you from a reactive mindset to a proactive one, putting you in control of your focus and making it far more likely you'll end the day with a sense of purpose and joy.

M — Mindfulness

One morning, I walked to the San Gabriel River near my home and filled a Mason jar with muddy water. As I carried it back, the debris swirled inside. By the next morning, the particles had settled to the bottom, leaving the water clear. That jar became a daily reminder: my mind also needs stillness for the clutter to settle.

Psalm 46:10 says, *"Be still, and know that I am God."* Mindfulness isn't emptying your mind but creating stillness. It's the practice of being present in the moment, without judgment, and allowing your thoughts to pass without getting caught up in them. The Dalai Lama, in *The Art of Happiness*, teaches that cultivating inner calm is essential to lasting joy—not because it eliminates life's challenges, but by changing how we move through them.

Why It Works: Mindfulness activates the parasympathetic nervous system—your body's natural "rest and digest" mode—which lowers stress hormones, slows the heart rate, and improves emotional regulation. Research from Harvard University shows that mindfulness meditation can actually increase the gray matter in areas of the brain related to memory, learning, and emotional control. Other studies have linked even short daily mindfulness practices to reduced anxiety, better focus, and greater resilience in the face of stress.

How I Use It: For me, mindfulness often looks like a quiet early morning on my back patio—no phone, no TV, just a cup of coffee, and a few simple practices to center my mind and body. I'll start with a breathing exercise like Box Breathing (inhale for 4 counts, hold for 4, exhale for 4, hold for 4) or 4-7-8 Breathing (inhale for 4 counts, hold for 7, exhale slowly for 8).

Some mornings, I add progressive muscle relaxation—tensing and then releasing each muscle group from head to toe—guided by the Calm app. It's a simple yet powerful way to release tension, tune in to my body, and start the day calm, focused, and ready. These small rituals slow my mind, steady my heart, and prepare me to step into the day from a place of peace rather than pressure.

My Action Plan (MAP): Start with just 5-minutes a day. Find a quiet space, close your eyes, and focus on your breathing—in and out, slow and steady. If your mind wanders (and it will), simply notice then gently return to your breath. Over time, you can expand to 10, 20, or even 30 minutes. Think of it like strength training for your mind—the more you practice mindfulness, the stronger your ability to stay calm, present, and focused will become.

S — Stretch

I've learned that stretching isn't just for the days I'm playing pickleball—it's for *every* day that I want to start with energy instead of stiffness. A few minutes of intentional movement in the morning helps me feel more awake, limber, and ready for whatever's ahead. After recent rotator cuff and bicep tendon surgery, this practice was especially helpful.

As Dr. Beth Frates, who directs wellness programming for the Stroke Research and Recovery Institute at Harvard-affiliated Spaulding Rehabilitation Hospital, explains, *"Stretching can help wake up the body and improve circulation. It puts us in a more relaxed state, helping set the tone for a calm morning and day."* Even a short session can ease tightness from sleep, shake off sluggishness, and give you a head start on a more joyful, focused day.

Why It Works: When you stretch, you increase blood flow to your muscles and joints, delivering oxygen and nutrients that improve flexibility and reduce the risk of injury. Research published in the *Journal of Physical Therapy Science* found that morning stretching can also reduce stress hormones and improve posture—which in turn can impact your confidence and overall mood. Stretching activates your parasympathetic nervous system, helping you feel calm yet focused, while also signaling to your body that it's time to move.

How I Use It: I aim for 10-minutes of light stretching each morning. Sometimes it's static stretches—holding a gentle hamstring, calf, or chest stretch. Other times I'll do dynamic stretches like arm circles, walking lunges, or gentle twists to wake up my spine. I focus on moving slowly, breathing deeply, and paying attention to how my body feels. As my shoulder continues to heal, I'm looking forward to incorporating practices like tai chi, which blend gentle movement, balance, and breath in the same intentional way.

My Action Plan (MAP): Pick 3 stretches you enjoy and do them first thing in the morning. Move intentionally, breathe deeply, and don't push to the point of pain—stretching should feel like relief, not strain. If you can, stretch near a sunny window or outside for an extra mood boost. Over time, notice how your body feels looser, lighter, and more ready to take on the day.

S — Sunshine

One of the simplest ways to boost your joy each day is to step outside and greet the sun. Dr. Andrew Huberman, a neuroscientist at Stanford, teaches that just 10 minutes of natural sunlight before 10 a.m. can improve mood, increase alertness, and regulate your sleep-wake cycle. This simple habit signals your brain: *It's time to wake up and engage with the day*. And here's the good news—it works even on cloudy days. Natural daylight is still far brighter than indoor lighting, and your brain responds to it all the same.

Sunlight also triggers your body to produce vitamin D, which supports mood, bone health, immunity, and energy levels. Researchers at the University of Toronto have found that morning light exposure helps regulate circadian rhythms—the body's internal clock—leading to better sleep quality, improved mood, greater daytime alertness, and more refreshed mornings.

Why It Works: Morning light sends a direct signal to the brain's *suprachiasmatic nucleus* (SCN), the "master clock" in your hypothalamus, which helps set the body's daily rhythms. This signal suppresses melatonin production (the hormone that makes you sleepy) and boosts cortisol to give you energy for the day ahead. Studies published in *Sleep Health Journal* and *The Journal of Clinical Endocrinology & Metabolism* show that consistent morning light exposure improves mood, cognitive performance, and sleep quality.

How I Use It: Most mornings, I grab my coffee and step outside for 10 minutes. I often pair this with light stretching to wake up my body. No sunglasses, no phone—just me, the natural light, and a few deep breaths. On rainy days, or when work requires me to be in front of my computer first thing, I use a light therapy lamp that simulates sunlight (a great option for those living in places with long winters or limited sunshine). It's a simple ritual, but it makes a big difference in my mood and energy for the day ahead.

My Action Plan (MAP): First thing in the morning, step outside for at least 10 minutes of direct natural light (or sit in front of a therapy lamp if there is no sunshine). Let the sunlight hit your face, breathe deeply, and use this time to set an intention for the day or simply notice the world waking up around you.

S — Smile

It sounds simple, but smiling—even when you don't feel like it—can shift your emotional state and brighten someone else's day. Studies have shown that a Duchenne smile, a genuine smile where the corners of your mouth curl up and your eye sockets crinkle, signals happiness and authenticity, reduces stress, and fosters social bonding. When you see someone displaying a Duchenne smile, you are likely to naturally feel positive emotions for the person smiling. Additional research shows that even a forced smile can trigger the release of dopamine, serotonin, and endorphins—your brain's feel-good chemicals.

Here's an experiment you can try at home in front of a mirror: Place a pencil horizontally between your teeth, without it touching your lips, for 30-45 seconds. This motion activates the muscles used in smiling, sending a signal to your brain that prompts the release of serotonin and dopamine. Even though the smile starts out forced, your body responds as if it were real.

Forcing yourself to smile can make you feel better!

Tal Ben-Shahar, author of *Happier*, teaches that our emotions often follow our actions, not the other way around. In other words, if you act happy, your mood is likely to catch up.

And here's the beautiful part: smiles are contagious. Studies at Uppsala University in Sweden found that when we see someone smile, we can't help but mimic it, creating a loop of shared positivity. It's a simple way to lift the emotional climate in a room without saying a word.

Why It Works:: The *facial feedback hypothesis*, supported by studies from psychologists Fritz Strack, Leonard Martin, and Sabine Stepper, suggests that the physical act of smiling can influence your emotional experience. When the muscles in your face form a smile, your amygdala—the part of the brain that processes emotion—sends feedback that reinforces a positive state. This means you can literally "smile yourself happier," while also triggering the same chemicals in others who see you.

How I Use It: I make it a point to start my morning with a smile—sometimes in the mirror, sometimes toward Tracy, and sometimes just sitting with my dog Zoe on the patio with my coffee.

I like to take it a step further with what I call *Laughter on Purpose*: intentionally seeking something that makes me laugh every day. Whether it's a funny video on Instagram, a good dad joke, or a fun memory, laughter delivers an even bigger boost of feel-good chemicals and deepens our sense of connection with others.

My Action Plan (MAP): Begin your day by smiling—even if you don't feel like it. Challenge yourself to smile at three people before lunch. Add a daily dose of *Laughter on Purpose* by watching, reading, or listening to something that makes you laugh out loud. You'll be amazed at how this tiny practice can change the tone of your day.

My mornings set the tone for everything that follows. **JAMSSS** clears the space, sharpens my focus, and fuels my energy—but joy doesn't stop there. It multiplies when it's shared. That's why the habit I treasure most is kindness. More than any other practice, it bridges my private rhythm with the lives I touch each day. Research shows kindness is the single most effective way to boost our own happiness while lifting others.

Before we move into my list of ten proven Happy Habits, I want to pause here to highlight kindness—because it's the one habit that has profoundly changed my life.

"Be kind to one another, tenderhearted,
forgiving one another,
as God in Christ has forgiven you."
—Ephesians 4:32

Pass It On

I once heard a story that illustrates a simple but powerful truth about kindness. In the story, an elementary school teacher gave every student—from first through fifth grade—a balloon and asked them to write their name on it. All the balloons were placed in the hallway. Then the students were told to find the balloon with their own name. Chaos followed—they searched and searched, but only a few could find their balloon.

Then the teacher gave a new instruction: "Find any balloon with a name on it and give it to that person." Within minutes, every student was holding their own balloon.

The lesson was clear: sometimes the quickest way to find your own joy is to help someone else find theirs. As Buddha says, *"Thousands of candles can be lit from a single candle, and the life of the candle will not be shortened. Happiness never decreases by being shared."*

Kindness is one of the most powerful joy-boosters we have. Research by Dr. Sonja Lyubomirsky found that acts of kindness can increase happiness by as much as 46%. An Oxford University study found that people who performed small acts of kindness for others for seven days reported significantly higher levels of happiness. And it works both ways—it uplifts the one receiving it and the one giving it.

Adam Grant's research at the Wharton School also shows that when you give freely, you can influence your social network to become more generous. Kindness inspires kindness, creating a ripple effect that spreads far beyond the initial act. Remember the movie *Pay It Forward*, based upon Catherine Ryan Hyde's novel? It began with someone picking up a child's dropped doll, which inspired the mother to move a coffee cup out of harm's way, which prompted someone else to help a pedestrian who tripped. One act sparked another, then another—kindness is contagious like that.

George Burns says, *"The nicest thing you can do for yourself is to do something nice for someone else."* Proverbs 11:25 echoes the same truth, *"A generous person will prosper; whoever refreshes others will be refreshed."* And Micah 6:8 reminds us exactly how we are called to live: *"Do what is right to other people, love, being kind to others, and live humbly."*

Several years ago, when my daughter Kait was in high school, she went on a mission trip with our church to Guatemala. Their project was to help build a water well for a village that had long struggled with access to clean, safe drinking water. In many parts of Guatemala, families walk miles each day just to collect water, often from contaminated sources. The lack of clean water isn't just inconvenient—it can mean sickness, missed school for children, and daily survival struggles for families.

Kait and her team spent long days digging, hauling, and working alongside the local community. It was hot, dirty, and exhausting work. But when the well was completed, everything changed. Clean water was no longer a distant hope—it was right there in the center of the village.

I still remember Kait telling me how she had never felt so tired and yet so full of joy at the same time. What lit her up wasn't just the accomplishment of finishing the project, but of knowing her sweat and effort meant children would drink clean water, mothers would worry less, and families would thrive in a way they couldn't before. The joy she experienced was directly tied to serving others.

That's the secret of kindness: when we give of ourselves, we don't just refresh others—we end up refreshed too. Kait went to Guatemala to serve, but she came home changed. Helping others gave her a happiness that no amount of comfort or convenience at home could ever match.

Kindness doesn't have to be grand or complicated. It can be offering a genuine compliment, paying for someone's coffee, helping a coworker or neighbor with a task, sending a note of encouragement, or simply being fully present with a friend who needs to talk. Small acts create ripples you may never see—but those ripples often travel farther than you can imagine, touching people you may never meet. A kind word, a smile, or a simple gesture can brighten someone's day, influencing how they treat the next person they encounter. Over time, those small waves can grow into a current strong enough to shift the emotional climate of a home, a workplace, a community—even a life.

And it's not just about being kind to others. We need to be kind to ourselves, too. Many of us, including me, can be our own worst critic—replaying mistakes, second-guessing decisions, and holding ourselves to impossibly high standards. Maybe you've been there too. The truth is, if we spoke to our friends the way we sometimes speak to ourselves, we wouldn't have many friends left. Self-kindness means speaking with grace instead of harsh judgment, offering ourselves rest, instead of relentless pressure, and remembering that God's mercy applies to us, too. When we extend kindness inward, we create the margin and emotional capacity to pour kindness outward.

Sometimes the fastest way to find your own "balloon" is to hand someone else theirs. This week, look for one "balloon" you can deliver. Who around you could use some encouragement, a helping hand, or an unexpected smile? You never know how God might use your small act to set off a chain reaction of joy.

Kindness may be my personal favorite happy habit, but it's just one part of a much bigger picture. Joy multiplies when our habits work together—woven into our daily rhythm like threads in a tapestry.

"Joy does not simply happen to us.
We have to choose joy and keep choosing it every day."
—Henri J.M. Nouwen

Happy Habits

Joy isn't only about how we begin the day. It's about what we carry through it. Over the years, I've discovered a handful of habits that help me feel better, think clearer, and bounce back faster. None of them are complicated, but like muscles, they grow stronger with use. Dan Harris, author of *10% Happier*, puts it like this: you don't have to become a Zen monk—just aim to be a little bit happier every day. Small steps, repeated often, compound into something powerful.

And here's the good news: self-care isn't selfish. Dr. Carol Dweck, author of *Mindset*, explains that people with a growth mindset believe their abilities can be developed through dedication and effort. This fuels resilience and the kind of daily habits that lead to lasting joy. My friend Anne Grady, in *Mind Over Moment*, writes:

> *"Resilience isn't about bouncing back; it's about moving forward. It's the ability to create a pause between what happens and how you respond, so you can choose the thoughts, actions, and behaviors that serve you best."* Proverbs 4:23 echoes this wisdom: *"Above all else, guard your heart, for everything you do flows from it."*

Science agrees. A 40-year longitudinal study from the University of Illinois found that the happiest participants lived nearly a decade longer than the least happy. A Harvard School of Public Health review linked positive emotions to lower rates of cardiovascular disease and stronger immune systems—meaning happier people literally get sick less often. And Gallup research shows that higher well-being is tied to stronger relationships, higher productivity, and better sleep. Joy doesn't just lift your mood—it strengthens your body, fuels your relationships, and helps you thrive.

Here are ten proven habits that have made the biggest difference for me—and can for you too. Think of these happy habits like a menu—try one or try them all—and then reflect on which ones have the most positive impact on you.

Move Your Body

Your body and mind are a team—when you get one moving, the other follows. My friend Darren Val Hendricks says, *"Life's a lot like steering a bike—you don't stay balanced by standing still. You stay bal-*

anced by leaning into the turns and moving forward." Exercise isn't just for fitness—it's one of the fastest ways to boost joy. You don't need a gym membership, expensive gear, or a marathon training plan. Even a short daily walk can create a noticeable lift in mood and energy. On days I skip movement, I feel the difference in my focus and even my patience. When I'm active, I think more clearly, my stress level drops, and I sleep better at night.

Why It Works: Shawn Achor, in *The Happiness Advantage*, says exercise "acts like a gateway drug to happiness," improving mood, energy, and resilience. Even short bursts of movement can boost brain chemistry in ways similar to antidepressants. A study published in *The Lancet Psychiatry* found that people who exercised regularly reported 43% fewer days of poor mental health compared to those who didn't exercise. Walking in particular is a powerful, low-impact option — it boosts blood flow to the brain, increases energy levels, aids digestion, reduces anxiety, and improves sleep quality. A study published in *Frontiers in Psychology* found that even light physical activity in the morning can significantly boost mood and mental clarity throughout the day.

If you have trouble getting started (like I do sometimes), Achor's concept of "activation energy" is a game changer. It's the initial effort required to start a task or change a habit. His "20-Second Rule" says that if you can make a desired habit easier to start—by reducing the activation energy—you're more likely to do it. For me, that might mean laying out my walking shoes the night before so there's a visual reminder of the habit I'm trying to create when I get up in the morning.

I started with slow walks around my neighborhood during transplant recovery. At first, I was thrilled just to make it to the end of the block. Over time, those walks turned into pickleball matches with Tracy, and most recently, a 500-mile hike on the Camino de Santiago. These workouts push me to sweat, stretch, and feel alive. Moving my body changes my mood faster than almost anything else.

My Action Plan (MAP): Aim for at least 20 minutes of movement each day. For me, that's often a brisk morning walk or a few games of pickleball. If that feels like too much to start, try 10 minutes after a meal—it will help with digestion and mood. Build it into your routine so it's non-negotiable, like brushing your teeth. On busy days, break it into smaller chunks: park farther away, take the stairs, or take multiple 5 minutes walks around the office. Use the 20-Second Rule to remove barriers—keep workout gear handy, block time on your calendar, or invite a friend to join you. The key is consistency—moving your body daily keeps your joy in motion too.

Eliminate Joy-Drainers

Gretchen Rubin, in *The Happiness Project*, reminds us that sometimes the fastest way to feel happier isn't by adding more good things—it's by removing the things that constantly weigh us down. Think of it like carrying a backpack: you can keep adding small comforts, but if you never take out the heavy rocks, you'll still be exhausted.

One of those rocks was overcommitting my calendar. I used to say "yes" to almost everything — speaking engagements, meetings, volunteer opportunities—until I realized I was running on fumes and missing out on unhurried time with Tracy and the kids. Cutting back wasn't easy, but the freedom it gave me was worth it.

I embraced my word for the year, Yutori, a Japanese word

that translates to: *the conscious act of slowing down*. I also learned an important distinction: there's a difference between stopping something that no longer brings you joy and quitting something simply because it's hard. One frees you; the other robs you of growth.

The Bible gives us a beautiful picture of this in John 15:2, where Jesus says that every branch that bears fruit is pruned so it can bear even more. Pruning isn't punishment—it's a process of removing what no longer serves us so that what remains can flourish. In life, eliminating joy-drainers is a form of pruning. It may feel uncomfortable in the moment, but it makes room for healthier, more joyful growth.

Research backs up the power of subtraction. Dr. Leidy Klotz, author of *Subtract: The Untapped Science of Less*, found that humans have a bias toward adding more rather than taking away—even when subtraction would lead to better results. In life, that means we often tolerate energy drains because we're too busy chasing the next addition. Removing them creates margin—space for rest, creativity, and deeper relationships.

<u>Why It Works:</u> Joy-drainers consume your mental, emotional, and physical energy. By eliminating them, you reclaim bandwidth for the things that truly matter. Over time, this reduces stress, improves health, and strengthens your ability to say "yes" to the right opportunities.

<u>My Action Plan (MAP):</u> This week, make a "Joy Audit." List the activities, commitments, and even people that consistently drain your energy. For each one, decide: *Eliminate, Delegate, or Limit.* Then take one small action to lighten your load—cancel a meeting, set a boundary, or politely decline a request.

Savor the Small Wins

Martin Seligman, the father of positive psychology, teaches the importance of *savoring*—fully embracing the good moments in our day instead of rushing past them. Dr. Andy Cope, from *Being Brilliant*, calls it "finding joy in the little things."

For years, I thought happiness was getting LED headlights on my BMW or getting a surprise upgrade to premium economy on a flight. And yes, those moments made me happy — but the joy faded quickly. Over time, I realized the most enduring happiness often comes from things money can't buy: watching the sunrise, sipping coffee on the patio with Tracy, or having a one-on-one meal with one of my kids. Arthur C. Brooks, in *Build the Life You Want*, reminds us that appreciating small wins daily isn't just a nice idea—it's a skill we can learn and strengthen with practice.

That shift in perspective changed everything for me. I started looking for—and noticing—small moments of joy throughout my day. One practice that's helped is *100 Happy Days*—taking a photo each day of something that makes me happy, no matter how small. Over time, the photos become a personal highlight reel, proof that joy isn't rare; it's woven into the fabric of everyday life if we take the time to notice.

But here's the trap: Have you ever caught yourself thinking, *I'll be happy when...*?

- When I get a promotion.
- When I lose weight.
- When I retire.

The problem is that "I'll be happy when..." thinking pushes joy into the future—always just out of reach. Even worse, once we *do* get what we wanted, the boost often doesn't last. Psychologists call this the *hedonic treadmill*—we adapt quickly to new circumstances, so we immediately start chasing the next goal.

Joy isn't about ignoring your ambitions or pretending everything's perfect. It's about refusing to postpone peace until life lines up exactly how you want it. Paul wrote in Philippians 4:11, "*I have learned to be content whatever the circumstances.*" He didn't stop striving—he simply learned to bring joy with him on the journey.

Why It Works: Savoring strengthens the neural pathways that help us notice and remember positive experiences. Research by Fred Bryant, author of *Savoring: A New Model of Positive Experience*, shows that actively savoring—slowing down to notice the good—can increase happiness, boost resilience, and even counteract the brain's natural negativity bias. It trains your mind to scan for what's right instead of only focusing on what's wrong. Over time, this makes joy less dependent on big wins and more anchored in daily life.

My Action Plan (MAP): Today, pause for at least 15 seconds to fully take in one small moment you enjoy. No multitasking, no rushing—just *be there*. Notice what you see, hear, smell, and feel. The next time you hear yourself say, *I'll be happy when...*, stop and flip it: *How can I find joy right now, even if nothing changes?* Try capturing one small win each day—in a journal, on your phone, or with a photo—and watch how your ability to spot joy grows stronger over time.

Weightless

Music has a way of tapping into your emotional brain and speaking directly to your heart. It can shift your mood almost instantly—no pep talk required. One of my personal go-to's is the song *Weightless* by Marconi Union, which a study by Mindlab International found to reduce anxiety by up to 65%. The song was designed in collaboration with sound therapists to slow your heart rate, lower blood pressure, and calm the nervous system. You can find it on Spotify, Apple Music, or YouTube.

But music doesn't just soothe—it can energize, too. Sometimes what I need most is a high-energy playlist in the car, with the windows down. Certain songs can snap me out of a funk, help me focus, or set the tone for a great day. One of my all-time favorites *is Shiny Happy People* by R.E.M. Neuroscientists have found that listening to music you love increases dopamine—the brain's "feel-good" chemical—and activates the same reward centers as eating your favorite dessert or spending time with someone you love.

Why It Works: Research in Nature Neuroscience shows that music engages multiple brain regions at once, including those tied to emotion, memory, and motivation. This is why a single song can transport you back to a specific moment in time or stir up feelings you didn't even realize were there. Calming music, like Weightless, works by entraining your brainwaves—gradually guiding them into a slower, more relaxed state. Upbeat music, on the other hand, can raise energy levels, improve coordination, and even boost exercise performance. In short, music doesn't just reflect your mood—it can shape it.

My Action Plan (MAP): Create two playlists—one for calming and one for energizing. Include songs that have personal meaning, not just ones you think "should" make you feel a certain way. Use your calming playlist during stressful moments or to wind down before bed. Play your energizing list when you need motivation to start a task, power through a workout, or lift your mood. Keep them handy, and the next time you feel stuck, hit play and let the music do its work.

The Power of the Pause

A few years back, I found myself running on empty. I was saying "yes" to everything—speaking engagements, work projects, social commitments—and doing it all at full throttle. From the outside, it might have looked like I was handling it just fine, but my energy, patience, and joy was fading. Looking back, I can see it for what it was: burnout. It didn't arrive in a single dramatic moment; I slowly drained myself by never slowing down. I needed to embrace a concept coined by blogger Anil Dash: JOMO (Joy of Missing Out) is greater than FOMO (Fear of Missing Out).

I learned this lesson the hard way: peak performance requires intentional recovery. Without it, even the best efforts eventually decline. I've even noticed it on the pickleball court. If I play for three hours straight without a break, my shots get sloppy, my focus wanders, and my "pickleball wizardness" (which is already debatable) disappears. But, when I take short breaks to stretch, hydrate, and socialize, I come back sharper, more focused, and ready to play my best again.

Why It Works: Science backs this up. Dr. Andrew Huberman, a neuroscientist at Stanford, teaches that peak performance comes from oscillating between intense focus and deliberate rest. He calls this "ultradian rhythm"—natural cycles of 90 to 120 minutes of productivity followed by 10 to 15 minutes of rest. Your brain and body need these recovery periods to consolidate learning, restore energy, and avoid burnout. Without them, your performance—and your joy—will suffer.

Athletes know this well. Olympic training programs are

built around recovery as much as exertion. Your muscles grow and your skills sharpen in the rest periods between training sessions. The same is true for your mind and spirit.

Even Jesus modeled this rhythm. In Luke 5:16, it says, *"But Jesus often withdrew to lonely places and prayed."* He didn't wait until He was burned out to rest — He built pauses into His life and ministry to recharge and refocus. It is reinforced in Psalm 23:2–3 *"He makes me lie down in green pastures, He leads me beside quiet waters, He refreshes my soul."* Notice the order: He makes us lie down before He restores us. We often want the restoration without the rest—but one comes through the other.

My Action Plan (MAP): This week, schedule at least one intentional pause in your day. It might be five minutes of quiet before your next meeting, a walk outside after lunch, or simply putting your phone away for a half hour in the evening. Treat it like an appointment you can't miss. Over time, these pauses become fuel for your joy, not interruptions to it.

Forest Bathing

Forest bathing—shinrin-yoku in Japanese—is the practice of immersing yourself in nature through all your senses. It's not hiking for exercise or rushing to a destination; it's moving slowly, noticing the way sunlight filters through leaves, listening to the wind, and breathing in the scent of pine and fresh earth. The goal is to be fully present and let nature quietly restore you.

The practice of forest bathing is not limited to dense forests, it is about immersing oneself in nature and engaging all five senses in a mindful way. My friend Russ Sablatura is an avid fisherman and says, *"A day spent fishing is a reminder that nature's real gift isn't in what you take home, but in what it takes off your shoulders."*

Why It Works: Spending time in green spaces activates your parasympathetic nervous system — the body's "rest and digest" mode—helping lower stress, reduce blood pressure, and promote a deep sense of calm. Even short periods in nature can lift your mood, sharpen focus, and strengthen your immune system.

One reason is explained by Attention Restoration Theory, developed by Rachel and Stephen Kaplan at the University of Michigan. They found that our brains get mentally fatigued from constant "directed attention"—the kind we use for work, problem-solving, and filtering out distractions. Nature offers "involuntary attention," where gentle sights and sounds—like leaves rustling or water flowing—effortlessly hold our focus. This gives our directed attention system a chance to rest and recharge, restoring mental clarity and boosting our capacity to think clearly and creatively.

When life stalls my joy, I plan a walk on the trail in our neighborhood, turn off my phone (most of the time I don't even bring my phone—no music, no podcast, no scrolling—this is known as Quiet Walking). I pause. I smell, touch, look, and listen—allowing nature's rhythm to settle my mind. Not just for wilderness trips—this works in any green corner: backyard, garden, riverside, even under city trees.

My Action Plan (MAP): This week, find just 20 minutes—yes, just 20—to step outside in nature or a green space. Leave your phone at home or turn it off. Engage with one sense: listen for birds, feel the breeze, look at leaves shifting, or breathe in deeply. No rush. Let your mind and body rest in the simplicity of the moment. Let this ordinary interruption become a source of extraordinary peace and joy.

Seven Types of Rest

Most of us think of rest as simply "getting more sleep," but sleep alone can't refill every tank that life drains. Dr. Saundra Dalton-Smith, author of *Sacred Rest*, teaches that there are seven types of rest we all need:

1. Physical: Resting your body through sleep or a nap.
2. Mental: Giving your mind a break from constant thinking and problem-solving.
3. Emotional: Finding safe spaces to be authentic without pressure.
4. Social: Spending time with people who energize you (and limiting time with those who drain you).
5. Sensory: Reducing noise, screens, and stimulation to give your senses space to breathe.
6. Creative: Surrounding yourself with beauty and inspiration to refill your creative tank.
7. Spiritual: Reconnecting with God through prayer, worship, or stillness in His presence.

Neglecting any of these can leave you feeling drained, even if you're getting eight hours of sleep every night. That's because fatigue isn't always physical—it can be mental, emotional, spiritual, or creative depletion. My attorney friend Thad Spalding says, *"In the courtroom, clarity wins. You can't think clearly, argue persuasively, or fight for justice at your best if you're running on empty. Rest isn't a luxury—it's the fuel for every winning case."*

Why It Works: Rest isn't just the absence of activity; it's the presence of restoration. When you match the type of rest you take to the type of fatigue you're feeling, you recharge more deeply and more quickly. Giving yourself permission to step away—from work, from noise, from screens—allows your brain and body to reset. As Mother Teresa said, *"We need to find God, and He cannot be found in noise and restlessness. God is the friend of silence."*

I check in with myself regularly to identify which type of rest I'm low on. If my eyes feel strained and my mind feels cluttered, I'll take a sensory break—no screens, no scrolling, just silence or time outside. If I'm feeling spiritually dry, I'll step away for prayer, journaling, or reading Scripture. The key is to be intentional instead of waiting until exhaustion forces you to rest.

My Action Plan (MAP): This week, pick one type of rest you've been neglecting and schedule it into your calendar like an important meeting. It might be turning off devices an hour before bed, taking a slow walk in nature, or blocking time for quiet reflection. Protect that time fiercely—because your joy depends on it.

Contemplate Death Daily

If you knew you had only one year left to live, what would you do differently, starting today? I know it sounds strange, but one of the most life-giving habits I've learned comes from one of the happiest countries on Earth... Bhutan. There, people are encouraged to think about death up to five times a day. Not in a morbid or fearful way, but as a reminder that life is precious, fleeting, and worth savoring. The Bhutanese believe that by contemplating death regularly, they learn to appreciate life more fully.

It's the opposite of what most of us do. We push thoughts of death far away, as if ignoring it will keep it from coming. But when we acknowledge our mortality, it can change the way we live. It's harder to waste a day when you know your days are numbered.

Dr. Daniel Amen once said, *"Live with the end in mind. When I was in college, I took a death and dying class and wrote my own funeral. It was one of the most important assignments of my life, because when you live knowing there's an end, you can do a better job at making each day special."* That perspective can shift your priorities, deepen your gratitude, and help you let go of petty frustrations that don't deserve your time.

The Bible reminds us of this truth in Psalm 90:12: *"Teach us to number our days, that we may gain a heart of wisdom."* Counting our days isn't about fear—it's about perspective. It's about living intentionally now, not waiting for "someday."

Why It Works: Thinking about death brings your attention back to the present moment. It strips away the trivial and focuses you on what matters most. Psychologists call this *mortality salience*—the awareness of life's fragility—and research shows it can inspire people to live with greater purpose, deepen relationships, and make more meaningful choices. Instead of motivating fear, it can fuel gratitude, compassion, and urgency for the things that count.

I've learned to pause and view my life through the eyes of my future self—imagining my 90th birthday, surrounded by loved ones, reflecting on the impact I've made. That mental picture shapes how I spend my time today and anchors me in purpose. Throughout the day, I ask myself a simple question that Susan and Russell Hartsfield shared with me: *"Am I doing what I want to be doing in this moment?"* Research by psychologist Hal Hershfield at UCLA shows that when we feel emotionally connected to our future selves, we make wiser decisions in the present—choosing actions that truly matter over short-lived impulses.

My Action Plan (MAP): Spend a couple of minutes each day contemplating the reality that life is finite. Visualize a milestone moment, such as your 90th birthday, and consider what you would want to be true about your life by then. Let that vision guide your actions today—from how you spend your time to how you treat others.

Pet Your Pet

If you've ever had a rough day and found comfort in the soft fur of your dog or the gentle purr of a cat, you already know this habit works. There's something grounding about the way animals meet you right where you are—no judgment, no agenda, just presence. They don't care if your to-do list is unfinished or if you stumbled through a tough meeting; they're simply glad you're there. That unconditional acceptance has a way of softening the edges of stress, and science backs it up—the benefits come surprisingly fast.

Why It Works: Just 10 minutes of petting a dog or cat can lower cortisol, the body's primary stress hormone. Researchers at Washington State University found that students who interacted with animals for even this short period had measurable drops in stress levels. Rhythmic petting also stimulates the release of oxytocin —the "love hormone"—which promotes bonding, trust, and feelings of well-being. Pets also help reduce loneliness and can spark conversations with other animal lovers, creating a sense of connection and community.

I make time every day to connect with Zoe—whether that's tossing her favorite toy, rubbing her belly, or just sitting together on the couch (she loves watching football almost as much as me.) It's not about the length of time; it's about being fully present and letting that connection work its magic.

My Action Plan (MAP): Build in a "pet break" to your day. Even 10 minutes can shift your mood and lower stress. If you don't have a pet, visit a friend who does, volunteer at a local shelter, or spend time at the pet store. The goal is simple: be present, connect, and enjoy the comfort and joy an animal can bring.

Acts of Anticipation

One of the simplest ways to increase happiness is to give yourself something to look forward to. It could be a big trip months from now, a lunch date with a friend, a Saturday morning pickleball match, or trying a new coffee shop on the weekend. Anticipation itself triggers a dopamine release—your brain's "motivation molecule"—which boosts mood and energy long before the event actually happens. It's like giving your mind a small, healthy shot of joy in advance.

When you pair anticipation with learning something new, the benefits multiply. Every time you master a new skill, your brain forms fresh neural pathways—a process called *neuroplasticity*. This not only keeps your mind sharp but also brings a sense of accomplishment that fuels long-term well-being. Whether it's picking up a musical instrument, trying a new restaurant, or planning a short getaway with your spouse, doing something new or different wakes up your brain and enriches your days. Brad Kinard says, *"Half the joy of traveling is in the dreaming. When Terra and I plan our next trip, the anticipation fills our days with excitement and our hearts with connection."*

Why It Works: Studies in positive psychology show that the act of anticipating a positive event can be as mood-boosting as the event itself. Looking forward to something—even something small—gives your brain a mental "bookmark" of joy to revisit.

Pairing that anticipation with new learning engages the reward system in your brain, keeps you mentally flexible, and can even slow cognitive decline. The combination helps you stay both optimistic about the future and engaged in the present.

I make sure my calendar always has at least one thing I'm excited about—sometimes big, like our upcoming trip to Panama, and sometimes small, like a date night with Tracy. I also try to commit to doing something new, like walking the El Camino, writing an article, or trying a Pilates workout. The key is to write it down (or put it on your calendar) and plan for it, because half the joy is in the countdown.

My Action Plan (MAP): Before the end of this week, schedule one thing you can genuinely look forward to—and block the time in your calendar. Then, choose one new skill, a creative project, or a topic you'd like to explore in the next 30 days. Break it into small, doable steps, so you can start enjoying the anticipation today.

These habits aren't about perfection—they're about practice. Over time, they've helped me not just endure hard seasons but actually enjoy the everyday moments in between. You don't have to adopt them all at once. Just pick one, try it this week, and see how it shifts your mood, your energy, and your perspective.

William James says, *"The greatest weapon against stress is our ability to choose one thought over another."* Our habits shape our thoughts, and our thoughts shape how we experience life. And while these practices fuel our bodies, our relationships, and our outlook, joy doesn't rest on habits alone—it flows from something deeper: a connection with the One who gives joy in the first place.

"Follow your joy and it will lead to
God's purpose for your life.
Joy is the beginning of bliss in life."
– *Kathie Lee Gifford*

From Joyful to Prayerful

Joy is a powerful companion for life's journey. Joy lifts our spirit when the road is steep and renews our strength when the miles feel long. But joy alone isn't enough. Without direction, we risk running hard—only to discover we've been chasing the wrong finish line.

That's where prayer comes in. If joy is the fuel that keeps us moving, prayer is the GPS that keeps us on course—guiding, recalculating, and realigning our steps with God's will. It's like my Tesla. I can have a fully charged battery, ready to go, but without the navigation system, all that power doesn't mean much. Joy fuels the journey and prayer ensures it has a destination.

Left to ourselves, we can slide into self-reliance, relying on what we see and know in the moment. But when we invite God into the conversation, we gain more than guidance. We receive His presence to steady us, His peace to calm us, and His wisdom to direct us.

In the next chapter, we'll discover how prayer is not simply a ritual to check off, but a relationship to lean into—an ongoing conversation with God, who loves you, listens to you, and walks with you every step of the way. Together, joy and prayer create a life that is both energized and anchored, fueled and guided, moving not just anywhere—but toward the destination that God has designed for you.

Prayerful

ADJECTIVE:

Characterized by or inclined toward prayer; showing reverence or devotion.

Tony Evans

"Don't worry that you may pray poorly.
Worry if you won't pray at all.
Just Pray!
It doesn't have to be perfect."

Philippians 4:6

"Don't worry about anything;
instead, pray about everything."

Our Call to be Prayerful

In the last chapter, we explored what it means to be *"joyful always"* (1 Thessalonians 5:16)—because I believe God wants us to live a life filled with true happiness and deep joy. But joy doesn't come and go like a mood; it's a steady, rooted experience that grows from our relationship with Him. I've learned that joy isn't about having a perfect life—it's about knowing Who is walking with me through it.

So how do we hold on to that joy, especially when life gets tough? One of the keys is found in the very next verse: *"pray continually"* (1 Thessalonians 5:17). Prayer is a continuous conversation with God—a way to lean on Him and find strength, peace, and renewed joy. Some of my best prayers have been prayed aloud in the car, during a morning walk, or of my back patio—no church pew required. Brother Lawrence, in his classic *The Practice of the Presence of God*, put it this way: *"There is not in the world a kind of life more sweet and delightful than that of a continual conversation with God."*

If joy anchors us, prayer fuels us. It's the rhythm that keeps us connected to God in every moment. In this chapter, we'll explore what it means to live prayerfully, staying connected with God throughout the day, in every moment, and in every circumstance. Think of prayer as a key to unlocking joy, peace, and purpose in your daily walk. You don't have to be perfect or have all the right words. Just start. God's not grading your prayers—He's simply glad you showed up. Prayer is how we lean into His presence, and every time we pray, we're saying "yes" to joy.

"The more you spend time with Him
the more you will discover your purpose.
Don't live your life trying to chase your purpose,
live your life chasing God
and you will run into your purpose."
—Jenessa Wait

Prayer Happens

Prayer isn't confined to church buildings or Sunday mornings. It happens in the car on the way to work, around the kitchen table before a meal, behind the scenes before a big game, and in hospital rooms where hope and healing hang in the balance. Sometimes it's whispered. Sometimes it's shouted. Sometimes it's silent. But it's everywhere.

A Pew Research Center survey found that about 68% of people pray outside of formal religious services, and 22% pray weekly or monthly. That means prayer is part of daily life for millions—even for those who wouldn't call themselves religious.

I love how Psalm 145:18 puts it: *"The Lord is near to all who call on Him, to all who call on Him in truth."* That means there's no "right place" or "right time" for prayer. It's not about the setting—it's about the connection. My friend Claudio Karolczak Jr. once told me, *"Prayer isn't just about words—it's about presence. It's learning to be aware that God is with you every moment."*

Psychologist Sonja Lyubomirsky points to powerful data showing that people who regularly engage in spiritual practices like prayer and worship tend to be happier overall. A Gallup survey backs that up: nearly half of those who attend religious services several times a week describe themselves as "very happy," compared to less than a third of those who rarely attend.

Why is that? Because prayer is more than a habit or tradition. Faith connects us to deeper meaning and purpose, and prayer is the lifeline that keeps that connection alive. It's oxygen for our spiritual lungs—it keeps our faith breathing. Prayer is where we share our fears and hopes, express gratitude, and trust God with our needs. It's where we're honest and vulnerable—and still ourselves long enough to hear His guidance.

It's not about perfect words or polished speeches. Just like with a close friend, the most meaningful moments are often the unpolished ones. Prayer works the same way—sometimes messy, always real. And when we embrace it as a continual conversation, it becomes a path back to joy.

Research agrees. Studies in psychology and neuroscience show that regular prayer or meditation can reduce stress, improve emotional well-being, and increase feelings of hope and resilience—even when answers don't come right away. That may be why more than half of Americans pray daily, according to Gallup. Globally, billions of people in every culture and faith tradition engage in prayer, making it one of the most universal human experiences.

If we're feeling stuck in sadness, anxiety, grief, or busyness, prayer invites us to pause, lean in, and remember we're not alone. And when life is going well, prayer becomes our way of expressing gratitude, celebrating blessings, and staying connected to the One who gives them. Over time, that steady practice builds a joy that's not dependent on circumstances but anchored in faith. I've had days where nothing around me changed—but because I prayed, my heart did.

Lysa TerKeurst says, *"The reality is, my prayers don't change God.*

But, I am convinced prayer changes me. Praying boldly boots me out of that stale place of religious habit into authentic connection with God Himself." And C.S. Lewis said, *"I pray because I can't help myself. I pray because I'm helpless. I pray because the need flows out of me all the time, waking and sleeping. It doesn't change God. It changes me."*

Prayer isn't meant to be complicated or reserved for the "spiritual." It's our lifeline—like breathing for the soul. It weaves into the everyday moments as much as the big challenges. The good news? You don't need the right words, the right place, or the right background to begin. Wherever you are, just start talking to God. He's already listening.

"The connection is maintained by obedience and prayer.
To remain in Christ
and to allow his words to remain in oneself
means a conscious acceptance of the authority of his word
and a constant contact with him by prayer."
—Chaplin Merrill Tenney

Hi Mom!

My mom used to text me almost every day, before she passed away at the end of 2023. Sometimes it was just a quick "Hi," "I love you," or "I miss you." Other times she'd add something extra—like an invitation to come over for her homemade spaghetti sauce (and that was always a guaranteed *yes*). Her messages weren't long or elaborate. They were simple, personal, and consistent. It wasn't about the information—it was about the connection. Those little texts were her way of staying in touch, keeping our relationship alive, reminding me I was on her mind and in her heart. She didn't wait for something big to reach out—she just reached out because she loved me.

That's how I think about Paul's words in 1 Thessalonians 5:17, when he encourages us to *"pray continually."* He's not telling us to speak prayers every second of the day. He's inviting us into a way of living where prayer becomes as natural and constant as breathing—something we can't live without. Think of it like Wi-Fi. Your phone stays connected in the background, even when you're not actively browsing. You can send and receive messages, get updates, and respond instantly when needed. You don't have to constantly tap the screen to stay connected; the connection is simply always on. Prayer works the same way—keeping your spiritual signal active. You're always in range, always aware of God's presence, ready to "send a message" (pray), "download wisdom" (listen), or "receive a notification" (a nudge from the Holy Spirit).

It's like my marriage to Tracy. Even when we're apart during the day, she's still on my mind. I might send a quick text, smile at a shared memory, or just look forward to being with her again. She shapes my mood and influences my choices. In the same way, continuous prayer is about being in close relationship with God—talking to Him throughout your day, thinking about Him, smiling at His goodness, leaning on Him when something feels hard. It's not about formality; it's about closeness.

Like a loving parent, God delights in hearing from us. Our prayers don't have to be formal or polished—just honest, regular, and real. Prayer isn't an event—it's a relationship. It's an ongoing, open-hearted conversation with the One who loves us most. Just like my mom's texts, our prayers—no matter how short—are expressions of presence and connection. And here's the thing—praying continuously doesn't require more time—it requires more awareness. A whispered "thank You." A silent request for wisdom before a meeting. A pause to breathe deeply and invite God into the moment. A walk where your thoughts turn into prayers.

Prayer can be woven into our days like my mom's gentle texts—short, frequent, and full of love. And just like her messages brought me comfort and joy, my daily connection with God brings peace, guidance, and the deep assurance that I am never alone. As Psalm 16:8 reminds us, *"I have set the Lord always before me. Because He is at my right hand, I will not be shaken."* When we treat prayer as a relationship, rather than a ritual, we begin to experience God's presence not just in church, but in every moment of our lives.

"When you ask, you do not receive,
because you ask with wrong motives,
that you may spend what you get on your pleasures."
—James 4:3

Small World, Big God

When I was 10 years old, my parents took me and my brother to Disney World. *It's a Small World* was (and still is) my favorite ride. I loved the bright colors, the singing dolls, and of course the song—which is now stuck in my head as I type this. While we waited to board the boat, I noticed coins scattered at the bottom of the canal. When I asked my dad about them, he said people tossed in coins and made a wish. He reached into his pocket and handed my brother and me each a quarter. "Go ahead," he said, "toss it in and make a wish." So we did. I can't remember exactly what I wished for—probably cotton candy or a Chicago Cubs World Series championship—but I do remember thinking, *This is magic.*

Here's the thing: prayer isn't a wishing well. You don't toss your hopes into the water and walk away, hoping something magical will happen. It's the same with those too-good-to-be-true emails you might get—like the one I once received from a prince promising me millions of dollars. (Spoiler alert: I didn't get the money.) In life, when we're desperate, we can't rely on a prince from a foreign country or luck alone. Prayer is not a last-resort lottery ticket. It's not meant to be locked in a case that reads, *"Break glass in case of emergency."*

Paul tells us in 1 Thessalonians 5:17 to *"pray continually."* He doesn't say, "Pray when you need something" or "Pray only when life is difficult." He says *continually*—in good times and bad. When I look back on my life, I've definitely been quick to run to God when things were hard—in relationships, with my finances, and with my health. But I'll admit, I haven't always been as quick to pray when things were going well.

In her song *"Flowers,"* Samantha Ebert sings about bringing her questions to God in a desperate moment and later, in a tone of gratitude, thanking Him for keeping her there. It's a beautiful picture of prayer that begins in the struggle and ends with flowers blooming in the valley. Prayer isn't about tossing wishes into the air like random seeds—it's about planting them with intention, trusting they'll grow in God's good time and according to His good plan. And that's the beauty of prayer—it's not just for the desperate cry of *"God, help me!"* but also for the joyful whisper of *"Thank You, Lord."* When we only pray in emergencies, we miss out on the deeper relationship God invites us into. God longs for our prayers in both the dark nights and in the bright mornings.

Prayer isn't about tossing a coin into the water and walking away—it's about staying in the boat with God, talking to Him as you go, and trusting that He's guiding the current. Jesus modeled this in Luke 5:16: *"But Jesus often withdrew to lonely places and prayed."* Even in moments of calm, He sought the Father. That reminds us that prayer isn't only reactive—it's proactive, a rhythm that steadies our souls before the storm ever comes.

The question this story leaves me with is simple: Do we treat prayer like a wishing well, or like a daily walk with God? When we learn to pray in both sunshine and storm, our faith deepens, and we begin to experience God not just as Rescuer, but as Companion.

"We tend to think that if we don't shout loud enough
or use the right words, God won't hear us.
Prayer is not a performance;
it's the life of God in us talking back to Him."
—Oswald Chambers

Pray like a Tax Collector

When Jesus told the parable of the Pharisee and the tax collector in Luke 18:9–14, He shocked His listeners. The Pharisee—respected, disciplined, and admired—seemed like the obvious model for prayer. Yet Jesus said it was the tax collector—the most hated man in town—whose prayer pleased God.

The Pharisee came to the temple with confidence, but not

humility. He wasn't crying out to God; he was reciting his résumé: *"God, I thank you that I am not like other people—robbers, evildoers, adulterers—or even like this tax collector. I fast twice a week and give a tenth of all I get."* (Luke 18:11–12)

There's no confession in that prayer. No request. No dependence. Luke even says he was *"praying about himself"* (Luke 18:11, NIV). He wasn't talking to God—he was performing.

The tax collector, by contrast, knew exactly who he was. Despised for working with the Romans and cheating his own people, he carried the weight of shame. He stood at a distance, unwilling to lift his eyes toward heaven. Beating his chest in sorrow, he prayed a broken but beautiful prayer: *"God, have mercy on me, a sinner."* (Luke 18:13)

No polished words. No spiritual checklist. Just honesty and humility.

And Jesus delivers the punchline: *"I tell you that this man, rather than the other, went home justified before God."* (Luke 18:14)

Why? Because *"all those who exalt themselves will be humbled, and those who humble themselves will be exalted."* As Max Lucado puts it, *"Our prayers may be awkward. Our attempts may be feeble. But since the power of prayer is in the one who hears it and not in the one who says it, our prayers do make a difference."*

That's the heart of this parable—it's not about polished prayers, it's about posture. We've all heard (or prayed) words that sound more like performances, full of "Thees" and "Thous," as if God were impressed by Shakespearean formality. But the Bible tells us God isn't looking for perfection—He's moved by sincerity.

If we paraphrased these prayers into everyday language, they might sound like this: The Pharisee's prayer: "God, I'm fine. Nothing's wrong with me." And the Tax collector's prayer: "God, everything's wrong with me. Help me."

Fasting, giving, and studying Scripture are good, godly practices—but when they become scorecards for superiority, we've missed the point. Prayer isn't a stage for self-congratulation. It's simply a conversation with a gracious God who longs to hear from us.

In my own life, I've prayed both kinds of prayers. I've come to God with polished lists, expecting His approval. And I've come to Him at rock bottom, unsure of what to say, simply asking for help. It's the humble, honest prayers that draw me closer to Him.

The Pharisee's problem wasn't his good works—it was that he trusted them more than he trusted God. The tax collector brought nothing but faith. And that was enough.

Here's the takeaway: God isn't impressed by our credentials—He's moved by our confession. The next time you pray, don't stress about getting the words right. Just be real. Pray like the tax collector: short, humble, and dependent on God's mercy; knowing this is the kind of prayer that moves His heart.

"The earnest prayer of a righteous person
has great power and produces wonderful results."
—James 5:16

Island Faith

I once heard a story about two men whose "three-hour tour" at sea turned into a nightmare when a sudden storm capsized their boat. It was a miracle they both washed ashore on a small, uninhabited island. Cold, tired, and hungry, they agreed they needed to pray to God for help.

But they decided to take it one step further. Wondering whose prayers carried more power, they divided the island in half, each man taking one side and promising to pray separately to see what would happen.

The first man prayed for food. The next morning, he woke to find a fruit tree heavy with ripe fruit on his side of the island. The other man's side remained barren.

A week later, the first man prayed for a way to make life easier. The very next day, a crate of supplies washed ashore, packed with blankets, tools, and a fishing net. On the other side of the island, there was still nothing.

Encouraged, the first man prayed for more: a shelter, more food, and something to provide shade from the relentless sun. And, day after day, each request appeared, like magic. Across the way, his companion still had nothing.

Finally, the first man prayed for a ship, so he could leave the island. The next morning, a boat was anchored just offshore. Desperate to leave, he prepared to set sail—without the other man. In his mind, the second man didn't deserve any blessings, since none of his prayers had been answered.

But, just as the boat was pulling away, the first man heard a voice from Heaven: "Why are you leaving your companion behind?"

"My blessings are mine alone," the man answered. "I was the one who prayed for them. He didn't receive anything."

The Voice replied, "You are mistaken. He only had one prayer, and I answered it. Without his prayer, you would not have received a single blessing."

The first man was stunned. "What did he pray for?"

The Voice said, "He prayed that all your prayers would be answered."

This story may be fictional, but the principle is deeply biblical. Philippians 2:4 reminds us, *"Let each of you look not only to his own interests, but also to the interests of others."* James 5:16 echoes the same truth: *"The prayer of a righteous person is powerful and effective."* One of my favorite examples of this comes from Max Lucado's book *Before Amen*. He offers this simple, powerful prayer: *"Father, you are good. I need help. They need help. Thank you. In Jesus' name, amen."*

A prayer doesn't have to be long, to be powerful. Prayer isn't a competition. It's not about tallying up requests or comparing results. Sometimes the most powerful prayer we can pray is for someone else's blessing, even when we have needs of our own. As Janice Hughes says, *"Rich is the person who has a praying friend."*

I've found in my own life when I take my focus off myself and pray for others—especially in their moments of need—my heart softens. My perspective shifts. My joy grows. And often I end up receiving blessings I didn't even think to ask for.

So maybe the best prayer you could pray today isn't "God, help me," but "God, bless them." When we pray for others, we reflect God's love—generous, outward-focused, unconditional. In blessing others, we often discover we've been blessed too.

"Now to him who is able to do immeasurably more
than all we ask or imagine,
according to his power that is at work within us."
—Ephesians 3:20

The Candy Man Can

When I was a kid growing up in Forest Park, IL, my dad would take me to Farrell's Ice Cream Parlour, on special occasions. It was an old-fashioned spot in a strip mall, with a soda fountain, big sundaes served in tall glass dishes, and rows and rows of candy in jars that seemed to stretch on forever. At the time, it felt like walking into a dream.

Those trips to Farrell's remind me of a story I once heard...

A boy named Greg went with his mother to an old-time drug store on Main Street. While she shopped, Greg stood frozen in front of the candy counter—wide-eyed, jaw dropped, completely mesmerized by the colorful display. The store owner spotted him and said, "Go ahead, son—grab yourself a free handful."

Greg didn't move.

His mom encouraged him, "Go on, it's okay."

Still nothing.

Finally, the owner reached into the jar himself, scooped out a generous handful, and poured it into a bag for Greg.

On the way home, his mom asked, "Why didn't you take the candy when he offered it to you?"

Greg grinned. "Because his hands are bigger than mine."

I get that. God's hands are so much bigger than mine—and He can do so much more in my life than I could ever manage on my own.

Too often, I've grabbed for what I thought I needed—prayed for what I wanted—only to find that my handful came up short. But, when I wait on God, His timing, His provision, and His wisdom, it always proves better. He fills my life with more than I could have imagined—not always more stuff, but more peace, more clarity, more joy, and more of what truly matters.

Ephesians 3:20 reminds us that God *"is able to do immeasurably more than all we ask or imagine, according to His power that is at work within us."* Our job isn't to figure out how much we can hold—

it's to keep our hands open so He can fill them. And that's the lesson prayer teaches us: God's hands are always bigger. When we trust His timing, instead of clinging to our own, we experience not just answered requests, but a deeper faith that rests in His abundance. The question isn't whether God is willing to give—it's whether our hands are open to receive.

"And above all this pray to the most High,
that he will direct thy way in truth."
—Ecclesiasticus 37:15

Big Mac Prayer

I was preaching a sermon on prayer one Sunday morning while my son Kip—just 10-years-old at the time—sat in the congregation. I shared about the power of starting and ending your day with prayer. Before your feet even hit the floor, you can whisper a simple prayer to begin the day with purpose and surrender. And then at night, just before bed, you can close the day with gratitude and reflection.

I called it a *prayer sandwich*—starting and ending your day with God.

Right in the middle of the sermon, Kip raised his hand and said, "Dad, you should call it a Big Mac prayer!" I paused and asked what he meant. He grinned and said, "You know—pray in the morning, pray at night, and pray in the middle of the day—just like the Big Mac has that extra slice of bread in the middle."

The congregation laughed—and I just smiled, proud of my son's insight. Kip's Big Mac Prayer idea is actually a beautiful picture of what Paul writes in 1 Thessalonians 5:17: *"Pray without ceasing."*

Morning and evening prayers are anchors, but that middle-of-the-day check-in—that extra slice—can be a game-changer. It doesn't have to be long or perfect. Just a pause. A deep breath. A whispered, *"Lord, I need You,"* or *"Thank You for walking with me."*

Those midday prayers can steady you when the day goes off track, calm your mind when stress creeps in, and pull your focus back when life gets noisy. Prayer was never meant to be a box you check—it's a rhythm. A relationship. An ongoing conversation with God, from the moment you wake up to the time you lay your head down at night.

Tomorrow, give the Big Mac Prayer a try. Start the day with a quick prayer before your feet even hit the floor, pause again at midday to re-center your heart, and finish with a prayer of gratitude as you close your eyes at night.

Three simple moments. One steady rhythm. A deeper connection with the God who loves you and walks with you through it all. And here's the takeaway: Prayer doesn't have to be long to be powerful—it just needs to be consistent. By inviting God into the ordinary moments of morning, midday, and night, you'll discover that He's already there, ready to strengthen, guide, and remind you that you're never alone.

\|/

"You were made to live in the kingdom of God, and that life is available to you now."
—Dallas Willard

Break Loose

Several years ago, Tracy and I were visiting the Lincoln Park Zoo in Chicago. While watching the elephants, I was reminded of a story I've heard over the years—often referred to as the *"baby elephant" analogy*—used to describe how limiting beliefs are formed.

The story goes like this: when elephants are young, they are restrained by a rope tied to a post. The baby elephant pulls and strains, but eventually stops trying, learning it can't move beyond that boundary.

As the elephant grows older and stronger—more than powerful enough to break free—it no longer tries. The rope remains, but it no longer has to be strong. The real constraint isn't physical anymore—it's mental.

That image stuck with me. How often do we live with spiritual or emotional ropes tied around us—ropes we could break—if only we stopped believing we were stuck?

Prayer has the power to expose those false beliefs and loosen old restraints. God invites us to bring Him our fears, doubts, failures—and even the long-held lies about who we are. In His presence, He replaces those lies with truth. He shows us that the rope was never stronger than the One who lives in us.

Craig Groeschel once said, *"The lies we believe will hold us hostage, but the truth of God will set us free."* That's exactly what prayer does—it exposes lies and anchors us intruth.

So let me ask you: What rope is still wrapped around your leg? What story are you believing about yourself that no longer reflects the truth of who you are in Christ?

Prayer isn't just about asking for help—it's about seeing ourselves the way God sees us. He doesn't see helplessness; He sees potential, power, and purpose.

As Paul writes in Galatians 5:1, *"It is for freedom that Christ has set us free. Stand firm, then, and do not let yourselves be burdened again by a yoke of slavery."*

Sometimes prayer is the spark that gives us the courage to try again. To step beyond limits we thought were permanent. To live like the chains really are broken—because, in Christ, they are. The rope around your leg isn't holding you back. It's the rope in your mind. And prayer is the place where you break loose.

"Trust in the Lord with all your heart,
and do not lean on your own understanding.
In all your ways acknowledge him,
and he will make straight your paths."
—Proverbs 3:5-6

Biking with Jesus

This story has been shared in many forms over the years, and its original author is unknown—but its truth is too powerful not to share.

At first, I saw God as a distant figure—like a judge, keeping score of my mistakes to determine whether I'd earned Heaven or Hell when I died. He was "up there," kind of like a president. I knew His name, but I didn't really know *Him*.

Then I met Jesus.

And suddenly, life felt a lot like riding a tandem bicycle. At first, I sat in the front seat, and Jesus was in the back, helping me pedal. I set the course. I decided the pace.

I don't remember exactly when it happened, but at some point, He quietly suggested we switch places. I moved to the back, and He took the lead.

That's when everything changed.

When I was steering, the route was predictable—straightforward and efficient. I chose the shortest distance between two points. But, when Jesus started steering, He took me on wild detours: up steep mountains, through rocky trails, around sharp curves, and sometimes at speeds that made me hang on for dear life.

Sometimes I'd yell, "Where are we going?"

He'd just laugh and say, "Pedal."

At first, I worried. I second-guessed. I longed for the safety of my old, predictable path back. But slowly, I learned to trust Him. I stopped longing for safety and started leaning into the adventure.

When I was scared, He'd lean back and touch my hand—a small reminder I wasn't alone. Along the way, He brought people into my life who gave me gifts I didn't even know I needed: encouragement, healing, acceptance, joy.

When He told me to pass those gifts along, I asked, "But what if I need them later?"

He smiled: "Give them away. They're too heavy to carry."

So I did. And every time I gave, I received even more in return.

I'll be honest—I didn't trust Him at first. I thought if I let Him lead, He'd crash the bike or take me off a cliff. But I was wrong. He knows the rhythm. He knows when to lean into the curves, how to fly over obstacles, and how to handle sharp corners and steep drops. *He knows the way.*

I'm learning to stop overthinking, to stop controlling, to stop complaining. I'm learning to pedal—even in the strangest places. And most of all, I'm learning to enjoy the ride.

Because I know who's in front. And when I'm sure I can't go any further, He just smiles and says, "Pedal."

We weren't meant to navigate life alone—or in our own strength. As Isaiah 41:10 reminds us, *"So do not fear, for I am with you; do not be dismayed, for I am your God. I will strengthen you and help you; I will uphold you with my righteous right hand."*

Like riding tandem with Jesus, true purpose begins when we move from the front seat to the back, from control to trust. The ride may get wild, uncertain, or downright scary at times, but with Jesus in the lead, every detour has a purpose.

Your job? Keep pedaling. Stay faithful. And enjoy the ride.

Where in your life are you still gripping the handlebars too tightly?

What would it look like to let Jesus take the lead—and trust Him with the route?

"God is not looking for extraordinary people.
He is looking for ordinary people
who will trust Him in extraordinary ways."
– Hudson Taylor

Fishing with Jesus

One of the most beautiful things about the Gospels is how

Jesus meets people right where they are—often in the middle of their ordinary, everyday work.

For Peter, Andrew, James, and John, that moment happened on a fishing boat. They were tired, discouraged, and probably smelled like seaweed. They had fished all night and caught nothing. Then Jesus shows up.

In Luke 5, He gets into Peter's boat, teaches the crowd from it, and then tells Peter: *"Put out into deep water, and let down the nets for a catch."*

Peter's response is so relatable: *"Master, we've worked hard all night and haven't caught anything. But because you say so, I will let down the nets."*

And what happens? They pull in so many fish that their nets begin to break, and their boats nearly sink. That miracle changed everything—they left their nets and followed Him.

But here's my favorite part: there's a second fishing story, years later. It's after everything—after the crucifixion, after the resurrection, after Peter's heartbreaking denial of Jesus. In John 21, the disciples are back on the water, maybe wondering what's next, maybe just going back to what they know. Again, they fish all night. Again, nothing.

Then a man calls from the shore: *"Friends, haven't you any fish? Throw your net on the right side of the boat and you will find some."*

They obey—and suddenly, 153 fish are flapping in their nets. John leans over to Peter and says, *"It is the Lord!"* And Peter—true to form—jumps straight into the water to get to Jesus.

The difference between the two stories is striking. The first time, they hesitated. The second time, they recognized. Because once God does something miraculous in your life, it's easier to trust Him the next time.

Think about that. Maybe you've seen God show up—healing someone, providing a job, restoring a relationship, opening a door you thought was sealed shut. That first time, it took courage to trust Him. But once you've seen Him work, you know His voice. You remember what He's capable of.

You might not be fishing for actual fish, but let's be honest—we're all fishing for something: Approval. Security. Love. Significance. Healing. A breakthrough. A new start.

So, let me ask: What are you fishing for?

Luke 5:5 says, *"Because you say so, I will let down the nets."* Are you willing to cast your net where Jesus tells you, even when it doesn't make sense? Sometimes, the blessing is just on the other side of the boat.

Faith deepens when we remember the last time God showed up, and we let that memory fuel our obedience today. Trust grows when we act on His word—not because we see the outcome, but because we know the One who's calling us to cast again.

Where in your life is Jesus asking you to "throw your net on the other side"?

I am blessed to be a kidney transplant recipient, and while I put my life and faith in God, the experience was still stressful for me and my family. I know that I will need another kidney transplant in the near future, but I'm not worried or stressed about it this time around. I know what He's capable of.

"Praise the Lord.
Praise the name of the Lord;
praise him, you servants of the Lord."
—Psalm 135:1–2

Daniel's Powerful Prayer

Daniel is often regarded as one of the most prayerful figures in all of Scripture. Even under threat of death, he continued to pray—three times a day. He didn't compromise. He didn't hide. He didn't let fear dictate his devotion. Daniel knew that anyone who prayed to someone other than the king would be thrown into the lions' den. Still, he opened his windows, knelt, and prayed—just as he had always done.

In Daniel 6:10, we read: "*When Daniel learned that the decree had been published, he went home to his upstairs room where the windows opened toward Jerusalem. Three times a day he got down on his knees and prayed, giving thanks to his God, just as he had done before.*"

His prayers were not shallow or scripted. They were consistent, heartfelt, and deeply aligned with God's will. In Daniel 9, we catch a glimpse of his heart—crying out in repentance not only for his own sins but for the sins of his people. He didn't just pray when he was in trouble. Prayer was his rhythm. His way of life. He prayed for wisdom. He prayed for guidance. He prayed in praise and petition.

God honored that faithfulness. Because of Daniel's devotion, God gave him favor with kings, influence in a foreign empire, and prophetic visions that still stir hearts today. And it all started with a prayer.

Daniel's life reminds us that prayer doesn't always change our circumstances—but it always changes us. In a world filled with pressure, noise, and constant change, a disciplined prayer life becomes our lifeline. It grounds us. Shapes us. Sustains us. His example calls us to keep showing up before God—regardless of the outcome, regardless of who's watching, regardless of the cost.

As author John Baillie once prayed: "*Grant, O most gracious God, that I may carry into this day's life the mind and spirit of my Lord. For His name's sake. Amen.*"

Like Daniel, may we choose prayer not as an occasional act, but as a daily posture—one that shapes who we are and how we live. Prayer is not only petition, it is adoration. Sometimes it's pure praise—and that's where the word *Hallelujah* takes center stage.

If someone observed your daily rhythm, would they see prayer as a priority?

What might shift in your heart, your home, and your hope, if you prayed with Daniel's consistency?

Faithful prayer builds a resilient soul—and God delights to honor those who honor Him.

"He who obeys the command
'Rejoice in the Lord'
has a Hallelujah in his soul
every minute of the day and night."
—A. C. Dixon

Hallelujah

The word *hallelujah* is a Hebrew term that translates to *Praise the Lord* or *Glory to God.* It's more than a song lyric or a call-and-response moment during worship—it's a sacred declaration that has echoed across centuries of faith.

Hallelujah is a word made of two parts. *Hallel* means "to praise," and *Yah* is a shortened form of Yahweh, the covenant name of God in the Old Testament. Put together, it literally means "praise the Lord." When combined, *hallelujah* becomes an exclamation—an outburst of joy, gratitude, and reverence. It's not just something we say. It's something we live.

The Psalms are filled with hallelujahs, especially in Psalms 113–118, known as the *Hallel Psalms.* These were sung during major Jewish festivals like Passover, reminding God's people of His faithfulness and deliverance. When Jesus and His disciples sang a hymn after the Last Supper (Matthew 26:30), scholars believe it may have been from this very section—a hallelujah sung in the shadow of the cross.

And in the Book of Revelation, the word rings out again—this time as a roar from heaven:

> *"After this I heard what sounded like the roar of a great multitude in heaven shouting: 'Hallelujah! Salvation and glory and power belong to our God!"*
>
> —Revelation 19:1

That's the arc of hallelujah—from the wilderness of Israel—to the table of the Last Supper—to the eternal chorus of heaven. It's the same word on our lips today, linking our prayers with generations past and with eternity to come.

Leonard Cohen's song *Hallelujah* begins with the lyric: *"Now I've heard there was a secret chord, that David played, and it pleased the Lord..."* Drawing from Psalm imagery, it points to something deeper than music. King David—called a man after God's own heart—had a "secret chord" that wasn't just about melodies on a harp. It was the way he poured his whole heart into worship—whether in triumph or tragedy. David's life shows us that worship isn't about performance—it's about posture. A hallelujah doesn't depend on perfect circumstances; it comes from a heart fixed on God. It's a declaration that says:

"God is good. God is worthy. And I will praise Him still."

Even when life feels uncertain... even when your prayers seem unanswered... *hallelujah* is an act of faith. It's not just a reaction to blessings, it's a decision to trust God in the storm.

Research backs this up. Neuroscientists have found that expressions of gratitude and praise actually rewire the brain—

boosting dopamine and serotonin, the very chemicals linked to joy and resilience. In other words, hallelujah isn't just good for your soul; it's good for your brain. Praise literally reshapes how we experience life.

That's why hallelujah belongs at the very center of our prayer life. The truth is, we don't always know what to pray—but we can always begin with hallelujah: praise for who God is, not just for what He's done. Praise lifts our eyes above our circumstances and fixes our hearts on His unchanging character.

From there, we can explore other ways of connecting with Him. But before we move on, pause. Take a deep breath. Fix your eyes on Jesus (Hebrews 12:2). And simply say... *Hallelujah.*

The next time life feels heavy, remember this: your hallelujah might not change your situation, but it will change you. Praise has a way of softening fear, sharpening perspective, and strengthening faith.

Do you reserve your praise for the good days, or can you lift a hallelujah even in the shadows of uncertainty? Hallelujah is more than a word—it's a declaration of God's goodness in every season, in every circumstance.

"Cast all your anxiety on him
because he cares for you."
—1 Peter 5:7

God Box

In her book *Help, Thanks, Wow*, author Anne Lamott describes a practice she calls the God Box—a simple, tangible way to let go and let God.

It's as straightforward as it sounds: whenever something is weighing on her heart—worry about a loved one, fear about the future, a situation she can't fix—she writes it down, folds the paper, and drops it into a box she has set aside for God. That's it. No rituals. No perfect phrasing. Just writing it down and placing it in His hands.

I love that image. It's honest. It's humble. It's prayer in one of its purest forms—admitting, *I can't, but God can.* And for those just starting their relationship with Him, it's a beautiful place to begin. Think of it as becoming pen pals with the Creator: you write, He listens; you release, He responds.

The act of writing something down is an act of surrender. It's our way of saying, *This is too heavy for me. I'm giving it to You.*

It reminds me of something my daughter Kait used to do when she was in middle school. She had a set of tiny *Worry Dolls.* According to tradition, children would whisper their worries to the dolls before bed and tuck them under their pillows. By morning, the worries were said to be carried away.

Kait embraced that practice. If she was nervous about a test, anxious before a volleyball game, or upset about a friendship, she'd "give it" to the dolls before bed. Looking back, I see how similar that was to the God Box: the real power wasn't in the dolls themselves, but in naming the worry and letting it go.

In Christ, we get to take that same childlike release a step further—not just handing our cares to a symbol, but to the living God who actually carries them. As 1 Peter 5:7 reminds us, *"Cast all your anxiety on him because he cares for you."*

If you've ever been hesitant to pray because you don't know the "right" words, the God Box reminds you there's no such thing. Prayer doesn't need polish—it just needs honesty.

You can start your own God Box with something as simple as a small box, a jar, or even an envelope—just label it "God Box." Keep some paper or post it notes nearby, and whenever something is weighing on your mind, big or small, write it down. Don't overthink it or try to make it perfect—just be real. Then fold the paper, drop it in the box, and pray, *"This is Yours, now, God."*

The hardest part comes next: leaving your worries in the box. Resist the urge to "take it back" by worrying and obsessing, and trust that God can carry what you cannot.

Dropping that slip of paper isn't just an action—it's a reset. It's a simple, physical way of praying with your whole self, reminding your soul Who's really in charge. The God who spoke stars into place and carved out the oceans is more than able to handle whatever you've scribbled in your handwriting.

Philippians 4:6–7 says: *"Do not be anxious about anything, but in every situation, by prayer and petition, with thanksgiving, present your requests to God. And the peace of God, which transcends all understanding, will guard your hearts and your minds in Christ Jesus."*

That's the promise: peace comes when we hand it over.

We all have something we need to release—a strained relationship, an unanswered question, a health scare, a habit we can't seem to break, a future we can't predict.

Some people who practice the God Box go back years later and open it—only to find that God has answered, redirected, or carried those prayers in ways they never imagined. It's proof that what felt impossible to us was never impossible to Him.

What burdens do you need to hand over to God today? Write it down. Put it in the box. Take a deep breath. And remember—you don't have to carry it anymore. God's hands are far bigger than yours.

Sometimes prayer begins not with speaking, but with surrender. The God Box isn't just a container—it's a confession of trust, a small but powerful act of faith that says, "God, this is Yours now."

“Prayer delights God’s ear;
it melts His heart; and opens His hand.
God cannot deny a praying soul.”
—Thomas Watson

Learning To Pray

Prayer is a journey, and like any skill worth cultivating, it doesn’t always come easily. Many of us struggle to know where to begin, what words to use, or how to stay consistent. Even with the best intentions, our prayers can feel distracted, uncertain, or repetitive—more like stumbling attempts than flowing conversations.

At its heart, prayer is simply a conversation with God. But even the best conversations can stall without rhythm, structure, and intentionality—especially when life feels chaotic or when our hearts feel distant from Him.

One of the most helpful guides I’ve found comes from George Buttrick, a pastor and scholar who wrote a timeless book in 1942 simply titled *Prayer.*

Buttrick didn’t see prayer as a rigid formula. He understood it as a relationship—a cultivated friendship with God. But he also knew that even the closest friendships require time, attention, and a little structure to thrive. In his book, he offers what he calls “a simple regimen of private prayer”- a gentle rhythm to help people enter into communion with God through thanksgiving, confession, intercession, and quiet meditation. He described these not as laws, but as hints—practical on-ramps for when prayer feels unfamiliar or stale.

Buttrick’s rhythm begins with stillness—settling the soul in God’s presence. It moves into gratitude—naming specific blessings. Then comes confession—honestly naming sins and accepting God's forgiveness. Next is intercession—praying for specific people and situations. And finally, adoration and listening—reminding us that prayer is not only speaking to God, but also hearing from Him.

This approach resonates deeply with me. We often assume prayer must be spontaneous and overflowing with emotion, but there is a quiet beauty in structure. I think of it like the trellis in my backyard: it doesn't constrain the vines; it gives them something strong to grow on. Structure doesn't limit; it supports.

We're also given a powerful promise in John 15:7: *"If you abide in me, and my words abide in you, ask whatever you wish, and it will be done for you."*

But answered prayer doesn't always look the way we expect. Pastor Rick Warren explains there are four ways in which God answers our prayers:

1. Go: *Right request, right time.* God says yes, and the door opens.
2. No: *Wrong request.* God's love sometimes means protecting us from what we've asked for.
3. Slow: *Right request, wrong time.* God is orchestrating the details, and patience is required.
4. Grow: *Right request, but you're not ready.* God is shaping your character to match the blessing.

Prayer is not about getting everything we want—it's about drawing closer to the One who knows exactly what we need. As Timothy Keller once wrote: *"God will either give us what we ask, or give us what we would have asked if we knew everything He knows."*

When prayer feels hard, or awkward, will you give up? — or will you lean into structure and guidance to help you keep going?

Remember: prayer doesn't need polish to be powerful. Start where you are. God will meet you there.

> "Devote yourselves to prayer,
> being watchful and thankful."
> —***Colossians 4:2***

Prayers Pathways

Prayer isn't one-size-fits-all. Some days it flows with ease. Other days, it feels awkward, dry, or distant. That's where prayer structures can help—not as rigid formulas, but as gentle guides for your conversation with God. Think of these structures as spiritual training wheels. Just as runners lean on training plans and musicians practice scales, believers throughout history have relied on frameworks to focus their prayers and deepen their spiritual life.

One modern example comes from Pastor Chris Hodges, who teaches the Five Ps of Prayer to bring rhythm and structure to your prayer life:

1. The Priority of Prayer: Give prayer a place of honor in your daily rhythm, ideally beginning your day with God before anything else.
2. The Place of Prayer: Identify a specific location to meet with God, just as Jesus often withdrew to quiet places.
3. The Plan of Prayer: Pray with intention by deciding ahead of time who and what you'll lift up, much like Jesus gave His disciples the Lord's Prayer as a framework.
4. The Power of Prayer: Remember prayer is more than words—it is spiritual engagement, bold asking, and be-

lieving God for great things.

5. The Person of Prayer: At its core, prayer is about God Himself—the Father who loves you, the Son who intercedes for you, and the Spirit who comforts and guides you.

This structure isn't meant to be a checklist, but a starting point for making prayer a daily habit filled with purpose and focus.

Another simple but powerful pathway is Breath Prayer, described beautifully in Jennifer Tucker's *Breath as Prayer*. This ancient Christian practice pairs slow, steady breathing with short, Scripture-based prayers—calming the body while drawing the soul closer to God.

The prayer is divided into two halves: the first is spoken while inhaling, the second while exhaling.

For example, from Psalm 23:1 you might inhale with, *"Lord, You are my shepherd,"* and exhale with, *"I have all that I need."*

Breathing deeply engages the body's calming systems, while the words align your heart and mind with God's truth. In many ways, prayer itself is like spiritual breathing—inhaling God's grace, exhaling your fears. That image has always reminded me of the worship song *Breathe* by Michael W. Smith, which captures this posture so simply: a recognition that apart from God, we are empty—and with Him, we come alive.

You'll notice many prayers end with Amen. This comes from the Hebrew word *āmēn*, meaning "so be it" or "truly." To say *Amen* is to agree with the prayer and entrust it to God. The Bible is full of examples—sometimes even "double Amens" (Psalm 41:13, 72:19, 89:52)—a way of emphasizing agreement and praise. The final word of prayer is not doubt or uncertainty—it's confidence. "Amen" is saying: God, this rests in Your hands.

Each of these pathways is not meant to limit prayer, but to open new doors. They are tools, not tests. Guides, not grades. Or as Captain Barbossa stated in Pirates of the Caribbean: *"The code is more what you'd call guidelines than actual rules."* The same is true here—prayer structures are not rigid laws, but gentle guides toward deeper intimacy with God.

If you've ever felt unsure of what to say, or longed for a deeper connection with God, these models can be a lifeline. Try one for a week. Mix and match. See what draws you closer to Him.

The following pages offer a collection of time-tested and creative prayer structures to help you connect with God in different ways—whether you're expressing gratitude, confessing sin, interceding for others, or simply sitting quietly in His presence.

Prayer pathways remind us that God meets us in both the spontaneous and the structured. The point isn't the method—it's the meeting. Whether through the Five Ps, a breath prayer, or a whispered Amen, *what matters most is not how we pray, but that we pray.*

\|/

"Lord, teach us to pray."
– Luke 11:1

Prayer Models

Prayer can feel overwhelming if you don't know where to start. Even the disciples asked Jesus, *"Lord, teach us to pray."* Throughout history, people have leaned on different frameworks as guiding patterns to help them focus their hearts and minds.

As Charles Spurgeon once said, "*True prayer is neither a mere mental exercise nor a vocal performance. It is far deeper than that—it is a spiritual transaction with the Creator of Heaven and Earth.*" Below is a collection of prayer structures—some ancient, some modern, all practical—that can help you deepen your connection with God.

1. ACTS

(Adoration – Confession – Thanksgiving – Supplication)

ACTS is one of the most widely used prayer models, popularized in evangelical traditions in the early 20th century. It begins with worship, moves into confession and gratitude, and ends with bringing requests before God—offering a balanced rhythm of reverence, honesty, and petition.

2. PRAY

(Praise – Repent & Rejoice – Ask – Yield)

PRAY is commonly taught in youth ministries and devotional settings as a simple, memorable framework. It begins with praise, includes repentance and rejoicing, invites requests, and ends with surrender to God's will, making it approachable for both new and seasoned believers.

3. PAST

(Praise – Acknowledge Good – Supplication – Thanksgiving)

PAST appears in modern devotional guides and emphasizes gratitude before petition. By first naming God's goodness, believers are reminded of His faithfulness as they bring needs before Him, ending with thanksgiving that reinforces trust.

4. ABCD

(Adoration – Blessing – Confession – Desire)

ABCD is often found in spiritual formation resources and pairs reverence with bold asking. It leads believers through worship, acknowledgment of God's blessing, honest confession, and open-hearted requests, creating a rhythm of both humility and courage.

5. HEART

(Honor God – Examine Your Life – Ask for Help – Request for Others – Thank God)
HEART is frequently used in mentoring and journaling practices. It invites self-reflection and intercession, guiding believers from worship to honest evaluation, prayer for self and others, and gratitude.

6. STOP

(Silence – Thanksgiving – Offer Requests – Pray for Others)
STOP is a modern prayer model designed for busy lives. It begins with a moment of stillness, shifts into gratitude, includes personal requests, and concludes with intercession—making it especially practical for short prayers during daily routine.

7. Five Finger Prayer

The Five Finger Prayer is a visual model often credited to Pope Francis. Each finger represents a prayer focus. The thumb reminds you of family, the index finger points to teachers and leaders, the middle finger calls attention to those in authority, the ring finger represents the weak and suffering, and the pinky reminds you to pray for yourself last. Its simplicity makes it especially popular with children.

8. The Examen

The Examen, developed by St. Ignatius in the 1500s, is a daily reflective prayer practiced for centuries. It walks through five steps: becoming aware of God's presence, reviewing the day with gratitude, noticing emotions, choosing one moment to pray through, and looking ahead to tomorrow—helping the believer discern God's presence throughout life.

9. The Lord's Prayer Framework

The Lord's Prayer, given by Jesus in Matthew 6:9–13, provides a timeless model for prayer. Each phrase serves as a pathway: approach God as Father, worship His name, surrender to His will, ask for provision, seek forgiveness while extending it to others, and pray for guidance and protection.

10. BLESS

(Body – Labor – Emotions – Social – Spiritual)

BLESS is a holistic prayer model developed in church-planting movements.It encourages prayer over the whole person, covering five areas: Body (health), Labor (work and finances), Emotions (peace and mental health), Social (relationships), and Spiritual (faith). It is useful for both discipleship and evangelism.

11. TRIP

TRIP, from Tim Keller's *Prayer: Experiencing Awe and Intimacy with God,* offers four movements: Thanksgiving, Repentance, Intercession, and Purpose. Its simplicity provides both structure and depth, making it an accessible daily rhythm.

Prayer is never about getting the words perfect—it's about drawing near to God. These structures are here to help you focus, not to limit you. Try one or two this week. Let them become a pathway, not a script. Over time, what begins as a framework can become a natural rhythm of conversation with God. As Augustine once wrote, "*True, whole prayer is nothing but love.*" And that is the heart of every model—to guide us back to love for God and love for others.

"Prayer is simply talking to God like a friend and should be the easiest thing we do each day."
—Joyce Meyer

From Prayerful to Thankful

Prayer keeps us connected to God. Gratitude keeps our hearts open to Him. Without thankfulness, even answered prayers can fade into the background, and blessings can begin to feel like entitlements. Gratitude transforms what we have into enough—and more; it shifts our focus from what's missing to what's present, and from what we fear, to what God has already done.

I often think of the song *Gratitude* by Brandon Lake, which reminds me what this kind of gratitude really looks like—choosing thankfulness not because everything is easy, but because God is faithful.

As the Apostle Paul reminds us, *"Devote yourselves to prayer, being watchful and thankful"* (Colossians 4:2). Prayer and gratitude are inseparable companions—one draws us nearer to God, the other reminding us to rejoice in His goodness.

In the next chapter, we'll see how living thankfully reshapes not only our perspective but our purpose, filling our lives with joy and anchoring our faith in every season.

Thankful

ADJECTIVE:
Feeling or expressing gratitude;
appreciative of benefits or kindness received.

Oprah Winfrey
"Be thankful for what you have;
you'll end up having more.
If you concentrate on what you don't have,
you will never, ever have enough."

Psalm 95:2
"Let us come into His presence with Thanksgiving;
let us make a joyful noise to Him with songs of praise!"

Our Call to Thankful

In the last chapter, we explored what it means to be prayerful always (1 Thessalonians 5:17)—keeping a continual conversation with God, leaning on Him for strength, peace, and guidance. But prayer is just one piece of the bigger picture Paul lays out in 1 Thessalonians 5. Right before *"pray continually,"* Paul says, *"be joyful always"* (v. 16), and right after that he writes, *"Give thanks in all circumstances"* (v. 18).

Gratitude, like joy and prayer, isn't meant to be occasional or conditional. It's not reserved for the moments when everything is going our way—when the bills are paid, the skies are clear, and life is good. Paul's words challenge us to give thanks in all circumstances—not *for* all circumstances, but *in* them. That means even in seasons of uncertainty, disappointment, or pain, we can still choose to be thankful.

I've learned that being thankful is not the same as being happy. Happiness depends on what's happening; thankfulness depends on where your heart is focused. Gratitude is a deliberate choice, a posture that reframes challenges and reminds us of God's faithfulness. It shifts our mindset from *obligation* to *opportunity*—what Jon Gordon encourages when he says, *"Replace 'have to' with 'get to' and turn the complaining voice into an appreciative heart."*

The command to be thankful in all circumstances isn't about pretending life is easy. It's about trusting that God is good—even when life is not. In this chapter, we'll explore what it means to live with a thankful heart, why gratitude is one of the keys to a truly successful and fulfilled life, and how it can transform the way we see the world. You'll discover that thankfulness is not just good manners—it's a spiritual discipline, a source of resilience, and a pathway to joy.

"Give thanks not just on Thanksgiving Day,
but every day of your life.
Appreciate and never take for granted
all that you have."
—Catherine Pulsifer

Happy Thanksgiving

When Paul offered encouragement to the church at Thessalonica, he wasn't talking about turkey dinners, pumpkin pie, or football games. He was pointing to a posture of gratitude that holds steady no matter what life looks like. And yet, our national holiday of Thanksgiving paints a vivid picture of what that kind of thankfulness can look like in action.

The Pilgrims who landed at Plymouth Rock over 300 years ago had no idea of the luxuries you and I enjoy today. During that first brutal winter, they buried far more people than they built homes for and their daily ration was sometimes only five kernels of corn per person. And yet, during loss, hunger, and uncertainty, they still found reasons to give thanks.

That season was marked by hardship, loss, and complexity—but even then, this small practice offers a glimpse of gratitude formed in scarcity.

They even created a tradition of placing five kernels of corn on each plate before a meal. One by one, each person would pick up a kernel and share something they were thankful for. It was a simple but powerful reminder of God's provision—even when that provision seemed impossibly small.

Thanksgiving is unique among our national holidays. It doesn't mark a battle or a birthday; it's a day simply set aside to express thanks to God. In 1789, President George Washington issued a public proclamation saying it is "the duty of all nations to acknowledge the providence of Almighty God, to obey His will, to be grateful for His benefits, and humbly to implore His protection and favor." His words still ring true: gratitude is both a privilege and a responsibility.

God's people have been practicing thanksgiving for thousands of years. In the Old Testament, we find Psalm 100—a "Psalm of Thanksgiving"—calling us to *"Enter his gates with thanksgiving and his courts with praise; give thanks to him and praise his name."* The psalm isn't just an invitation; it's a blueprint. It tells us not only to thank God, but to remember why: *"For the Lord is good and his love endures forever; his faithfulness continues through all generations."*

Their story reminds us that thankfulness isn't about the amount of food on your plate—it's about the posture of your heart. That's the same lesson Paul modeled in his own life. And if anyone had reason not to give thanks, it was him.

"You are my God, and I will give you thanks;
you are my God, and I will exalt you."
—Psalm 118: 28

Thankful Paul

The Apostle Paul was marked by more hardship than most of us can imagine. He was imprisoned multiple times, beaten with rods, whipped, stoned, shipwrecked (three times!), and often left hungry, cold, and without shelter (2 Corinthians

11:23–27). He faced rejection from those he was trying to serve and betrayal from people he'd trusted.

And yet, read through his letters and you'll find that Paul's words are filled with gratitude. Over and over, he begins his writings with thanksgiving—not for his own comfort or success, but for the people he's writing to, and the work God is doing in them. He tells the Philippians, *"I thank my God every time I remember you"* (Philippians 1:3). To the Thessalonians, he writes, *"We always thank God for all of you and continually mention you in our prayers"* (1 Thessalonians 1:2). Even from a prison cell, chained to guards and uncertain of his future, Paul declares, *"Rejoice in the Lord always. I will say it again: Rejoice!"* (Philippians 4:4).

Paul's thankfulness wasn't based on comfort or ease—it was anchored in his unshakable faith in Christ and the joy of the gospel. His gratitude flowed from a deep awareness of God's grace, not from the absence of pain. He didn't wait for better circumstances to be thankful; instead, he let gratitude reshape the circumstances he was in.

Stephen Colbert once said, *"It's a gift to exist, and with existence comes suffering. There's no escaping that. If you're grateful for your life, then you have to be grateful for all of it. You can't pick and choose what you're grateful for."* That's exactly how Paul lived. He understood that if you're going to thank God for the blessings, you must also thank Him in the battles. Gratitude isn't a selective response; it's an all-in way of life.

This is one of the great lessons of Paul's story: thankfulness flows from relationship, not circumstance. When our hearts are rooted in Christ, we can see blessings in places where others see only hardship. Paul's attitude turned prison walls into pulpits and suffering into a platform for praise.

"Gratitude is not only a response to grace;
it is the very condition in which faith flourishes."
—N.T. Wright

Give Thanks

Two thousand years after Paul wrote his letters from prison, modern research is proving what he lived out daily—gratitude really does change everything.

Dr. Robert Emmons, one of the world's leading experts on gratitude, has found that people who practice gratitude consistently report stronger immune systems, lower blood pressure, higher levels of positive emotions, more joy and optimism, and deeper relationships. Gratitude, he says, functions like a psychological immune system—helping us reframe setbacks, recover faster from adversity, and find meaning in difficulty.

And it's not just emotional. A study by Dr. Paul Mills at the University of California, San Diego, discovered that patients with heart disease who practiced daily gratitude had better heart health, lower inflammation, and improved sleep compared to those who didn't. Gratitude impacts not only how we think, but also how our bodies respond.

Harvard Business Review reports that gratitude not only makes people feel appreciated but also strengthens trust and collaboration in workplaces—environments that, like Paul's churches, thrive on encouragement and shared mission. In other words, thankfulness builds both resilience and connection, whether you're in a first-century prison cell or a twenty-first-century conference room.

Psychologist Dr. Martin Seligman also found that writing and delivering a letter of gratitude boosted happiness by around 10% and reduced depressive symptoms for up to a month—proof that taking action on gratitude amplifies its effect.

C.S. Lewis wrote, "*We ought to give thanks for all fortune: if it is good, because it is good; if bad, because it works in us patience, humility, and the contempt of this world and the hope of our eternal country.*"

Gratitude should not be selective. It doesn't just show up when life is easy; it transforms us in the seasons when life is hard. I've experienced that firsthand. On January 30, 2002, I received a kidney transplant. My donor was my brother, Don—an act of generosity and love I will never be able to repay. I remember waking up from surgery, overwhelmed with gratitude: for Don's gift, for the skill of the medical team, for my family's support, and for God's sustaining grace. That gratitude carried me through the long, sometimes painful, recovery. It didn't remove the difficulty, but it reframed it—every ache was a reminder that I'd been given more time, more life, more opportunity to serve.

"Some people grumble that roses have thorns;
I am grateful that thorns have roses."
—Alphonse Karr

Unlikely Gratitude

Gratitude often comes easily in seasons of blessing. It's much harder—sometimes painfully so—when life hands all of us disappointment. I've wrestled with Paul's command to *"give thanks in all circumstances,"* more than once.

I struggled to be thankful when our family moved from Chicago to Austin, Texas, leaving behind everything familiar. I sure wasn't thankful when I didn't make the basketball team back in high school, when I failed a college course, when I got dumped by a girlfriend, or when I lost a significant amount of money in the stock market. I wasn't thankful when I learned I needed a kidney transplant, or when the long-term medications from that transplant led to both of my hips being replaced. And it was painful trying to be thankful when my best friend and business partner and I decided we needed to part ways. I have a long list of setbacks and disappointments that didn't feel like blessings in the moment. Maybe you have a list like that too.

None of those moments inspired an immediate "thank you" prayer. And yet, with time and perspective, God gently showed me that thankfulness isn't about denying our pain—it's about anchoring our hope. Gratitude doesn't erase the loss or the disappointment, but it keeps our hearts tethered to the One who can redeem even the hardest chapters of our story.

One of the most beautiful flowers grows out of a cactus. In the same way, gratitude often blooms in unlikely places—in deserts of loss, frustration, or failure. Try asking yourself: *What is the unlikely gratitude in this situation?* And instead of seeing setbacks as dead ends, try viewing them as steps on a ladder. Health challenges can deepen compassion. Missed opportunities can sharpen focus. Relationship struggles can grow resilience and wisdom.

Psychologists call this *post-traumatic growth*—the idea that the hardest seasons can produce the deepest growth in a person. Researchers Richard Tedeschi and Lawrence Calhoun found that people who endure great difficulty often emerge with a greater appreciation for life, stronger relationships, and even deeper faith. Gratitude doesn't mean denying the pain; it means reframing the pain as a potential pathway for growth. As Dr. Emmons writes, *"Gratitude has the power to heal, to energize, and to transform lives."*

Arthur Brooks suggests asking 3 questions after a setback:

1. In the moment: What happened?
2. One month later: What did you learn?
3. Three months later: How did it benefit you?

I saw this play out clearly when my business partner and I made the difficult decision to part ways in 2019. In the moment, it felt like disappointment and loss. A month later, I could begin to name what I was learning—hard truths about burnout, communication, and the importance of alignment. Over time, I began to see how the experience redirected my work toward something more authentic—more life-giving. The pain didn't disappear, but gratitude slowly took its place.

With time, gratitude shifts our perspective. As Ann Voskamp reminds us, *"When we give thanks in all things, we get joy in all things."* Gratitude doesn't just change how we see the past—it transforms how we walk through the present.

"A complaining tongue reveals an ungrateful heart."
—William Arthur Ward

There's No Crying in Baseball

Complaining comes naturally to all of us. It's easy to focus on what's wrong, what we don't have, and what didn't go our way. And let's be honest—who really enjoys being around a person who always complains? But, if gratitude is said to be like water for the soul, complaining is like poison. It drains our joy, erodes our perspective, and trains our mind to look for problems, instead of blessings.

Psychologists call this the negativity bias—our tendency to dwell on the bad more than the good. Dr. Rick Hanson puts it this way: *"The brain is like Velcro for negative experiences but Teflon for positive ones."* It's part of human survival wiring, but if left unchecked, it can trap us in a negative cycle of complaint.

It makes me think of the famous line from the movie A League of Their Own. Tom Hanks' character shouts, *"There's no crying in baseball!"*, to toughen up his players. When it comes to a life of faith, I think Paul might have said something similar: *"There's no complaining in gratitude!"*

Science backs this up. Neuroscientists tell us that the more we complain, the more we wire our brains to see the negative. At Stanford, researchers found that habitual complaining can even shrink the hippocampus—the part of the brain responsible for memory and problem-solving. But gratitude does the opposite: it rewires the brain by activating the prefrontal cortex and releasing dopamine and serotonin, helping us notice blessings, opportunities, and reasons to hope.

Will Bowen, in his book *A Complaint Free World,* makes it practical: *"Complaining is like bad breath—you notice it when it comes out of somebody else's mouth, but not when it comes out of your own."*

Philippians 2:14–15 puts it plainly: *"Do everything without grumbling or arguing, so that you may become blameless and pure, children of God without fault in a warped and crooked generation. Then you will shine among them like stars in the sky."* Paul wasn't just giving moral advice; he was showing us that gratitude and complaining can't coexist. One dims the light of our witness, and the other makes it shine brighter.

Here's a simple challenge: try going 24 hours without complaining. No griping about traffic. No rolling your eyes at work frustrations. No moaning about the weather. And definitely no whining in the direction of your spouse (I'm sure you've heard the saying: "happy spouse, happy house"). I'd like to believe that I don't complain too much, but my wife Tracy laughed out loud when I asked her. When you catch yourself starting to complain, stop and replace that complaint with something you're thankful for, instead. It sounds simple, but it's harder than you think—and more powerful than you imagine.

Because gratitude and complaining are like two opposing teams on the field of your mind, but you get to choose which one wins the game.

"Develop an attitude of gratitude,
and give thanks for everything that happens to you,
knowing that every step forward
is a step toward achieving something
bigger and better."
—***Brian Tracy***

Attitude of Gratitude

Gratitude is more powerful when it's not just an occasional response but a way of life. It's not something we turn on in November as we approach the Thanksgiving holiday, or when things are going well. It's a posture of the heart—a daily choice to see life as a gift.

A few years ago, when we started building the house we live in now, I loved checking in on the progress and chatting with the workers. When I talked with the folks pouring concrete for the foundation, a few of them admitted they couldn't wait for the job to be finished so they could get paid. When I chatted with the guy installing the cabinets, he told me he hated his job, but it paid the bills, and he worked quickly to get it over with. Honestly, I could relate—I've had seasons where I grumbled about work, too.

But then I met Antonio, the man responsible for texture and paint. His perspective was entirely different. When I asked what he was doing, he smiled and said, "I'm preparing a home for the family that will move into this house." Antonio wasn't just painting walls—he was shaping someone's future. His gratitude transformed his work into something meaningful. I walked away thinking, *that's the attitude I want in my own life.*

Nhat Hanh put it this way: "*When we live in the spirit of gratitude, there will be much happiness in our life.*" That's the essence of thankfulness as a lifestyle—choosing appreciation over entitlement, perspective over complaints.

The Bible puts it even more clearly: "*Whatever you do, whether in word or deed, do it all in the name of the Lord Jesus, giving thanks to God the Father through him*" (Colossians 3:17). Gratitude is not about what you're doing—it's about how you do it. The same task can either drain you or fulfill you, depending on the spirit you bring to it.

Even science backs this up. Dr. Michael McCullough, a leading gratitude researcher at the University of Miami, has found that people who cultivate gratitude aren't just happier—they actually make better decisions and show greater self-control. Gratitude helps us focus on long-term goals rather than short-term impulses. It shifts our attention from what we lack to what truly matters, giving us both perspective and discipline.

Gratitude doesn't just change your mood—it changes your direction. It guides your choices, strengthens your relationships, and focuses your life on what really matters. That's why Paul could write, "*Give thanks in all circumstances*" (1 Thessalonians 5:18). He wasn't asking us to feel grateful only when life looks good. He was calling us to adopt gratitude as a way of life, a lens through which everything else is seen.

"Attitude of gratitude" is more than a catchy phrase. It's a habit of the heart. And when gratitude becomes your default, everything else begins to look different—your work, your relationships, even your hardships.

"Never lose an opportunity of seeing anything beautiful, for beauty is God's handwriting."

—Ralph Waldo Emerson

Knockout Roses

Tracy loves roses. A couple of years ago, she bought two pots of beautiful knockout roses and set them on our front porch. They looked great—at least for a while. But since I usually go in and out through the garage, I rarely saw them. Out of sight, out of mind. I forgot to water them, and eventually, they withered and died.

It wasn't that the roses weren't beautiful. It wasn't that they didn't have potential. They simply didn't survive, because they were neglected. I couldn't appreciate what I didn't take time to notice.

On the other hand, we also have knockout roses on our back porch—the place where Tracy and I sit almost every morning with our coffee. Those roses are thriving. Why? Because we see them every day. We enjoy their beauty. And, because they're on our radar, they get watered, pruned, and cared for. The difference wasn't the roses—it was the attention we gave them.

Gratitude works the same way. The blessings we notice are the ones that flourish. The ones we ignore are the ones that wither. When we pay attention to God's goodness in our lives—even in small, ordinary ways—our gratitude grows, and with it, our joy.

Colossians 3:15 says, *"Let the peace of Christ rule in your hearts... and be thankful."*

Gratitude requires intentionality. We need to pause, notice, and give thanks. Because what we water with gratitude will flourish.

"Instructions for living a life:
Pay attention.
Be astonished.
Tell about it."

—Mary Oliver

The Magnificent Strawberry

There's an old Zen parable about a man who was traveling

across a field when he was suddenly chased by a tiger. He ran until he came to the edge of a cliff, where he grabbed the root of a wild vine and swung himself over the edge. The tiger prowled above, waiting. When the man looked down, he saw another tiger below, ready to devour him.

As if that weren't enough, two mice—one white and one black—began gnawing at the vine that held him, slowly wearing away at his life. His grip was failing. His escape seemed impossible.

Then he saw it: a single, wild strawberry growing from the cliff face. With one hand clinging to the vine, he reached out with the other, plucked the strawberry, and put it in his mouth. How incredibly sweet it tasted.

This story is more than a tale of survival. The symbols hold meaning:

- ❧ The tiger above represents the struggles and fears of our present reality.
- ❧ The tiger below represents the inevitability of death that awaits us all.
- ❧ The two mice symbolize the passage of time, day (white) and night (black).
- ❧ The strawberry represents the blessings and joys available to us right now.

Life will always bring its share of "tigers and mice"—challenges pressing in from above, fears lurking below, and the steady wear of time. Yet, even here, gratitude invites us to pause and savor the "strawberries" God places on our path. Thankfulness isn't about escaping hardship; it's about noticing and delighting in the sweetness of life in this very moment.

The psalmist captured this truth: *"Taste and see that the Lord is good; blessed is the one who takes refuge in him"* (Psalm 34:8). Gratitude opens our eyes to see and our hearts to savor goodness. The problems may remain, but thankfulness keeps us from missing the blessings that are already there.

What magnificent strawberries has God placed within your reach today?

"When you change the way you look at things,
the things you look at change."
—Dr. Wayne Dyer

Gold Miners

One of my favorite questions to ask during a keynote presentation is: What do gold miners look for?

Sometimes people try to overthink the answer, but usually someone gets it right away: gold.

Then I follow up: "What do gold miners actually find the most, while searching for gold?"

The answer is dirt and rocks.

Finally, I ask: "What do miners do with the dirt and rocks?"

They toss them aside—because they're not there for dirt; they're there for gold.

It's a simple illustration, but it mirrors how we often live our lives. Too often, we find ourselves looking for dirt—what's wrong with the situation, what's frustrating about our job, what's disappointing about a friend or spouse. Neuroscience tells us this negativity bias—the brain's natural tendency to focus on problems, threats, and shortcomings more than blessings, opportunities, and strengths—was useful for survival in ancient times, but today it can be harmful.

Gratitude retrains our minds. It doesn't deny there's dirt—it simply helps us see the gold.

Philippians 4:8 gives us the blueprint: *"Whatever is true, whatever is noble, whatever is right, whatever is pure, whatever is lovely, whatever is admirable—if anything is excellent or praiseworthy—think about such things."* Paul wasn't saying to pretend the dirt doesn't exist. He was reminding us to focus on the gold.

The shift is subtle but powerful. Instead of asking, *What's wrong here?* you begin asking, *What's right?* Instead of fixating on someone's flaws, you notice their strengths. Instead of obsessing over obstacles, you look for opportunities.

During my hike on El Camino de Santiago, we experienced a downpour. It would've been easy to focus on the lousy conditions, my soaked clothing and shoes. Instead, I focused on the beautiful vistas shrouded in clouds and fog, and was thankful for the cooler temperatures.

Life will always contain dirt and rocks. We don't have to deny them, but we also don't have to hold onto them. Gratitude is the discipline of tossing the dirt aside and choosing to see the gold. The more we practice it, the more gold we'll find.

> "The way you see the world
> creates the world you see."
> —***Mel Robbins***

The Jeep Effect

A couple of years ago, Tracy bought a Jeep Cherokee. We'd

never owned a Jeep before. On the drive home from the dealership, I suddenly started noticing how many Jeeps were on the road. Every few minutes, I'd blurt out, "Jeep!" (probably to Tracy's annoyance). Before that day, I hardly ever noticed them. What changed? My brain had been primed—specifically, the Reticular Activating System (RAS). Did something similar happen the last time you bought a new car?

The RAS is a bundle of nerves at the base of our brainstem that acts like a filter, deciding which pieces of the world around us deserve our attention. With millions of sensory inputs bombarding us every second, most are screened out. But once something becomes important to us—like a new Jeep—our RAS starts flagging it everywhere we go. The world didn't change; our awareness did.

Life works the same way. What we focus on is what we'll consistently notice. If we dwell on complaints, frustrations, or fears, our RAS will faithfully deliver more of the same. But, if we train it to notice gratitude, blessings, and God's goodness, our mind begins to filter the world differently—we'll start to see reasons to give thanks that we once overlooked.

I often demonstrate this in my keynote presentations: I ask participants to look around, right now, and notice everything in the room that's blue. Memorize as much as you can. Now, close your eyes. Without peeking, try to list everything that was... *green*. Not easy, right? Because you weren't looking for green. Your brain was tuned to blue. Everyday life works the same way: we find what we're looking for.

Psychologist Barbara Fredrickson calls this the *Broaden-and-Build Theory*. Positive emotions—like gratitude—literally expand our awareness. They open us to new opportunities, more beauty, and deeper hope. In her words, *"Positive emotions broaden people's momentary thought-action repertoires."*

Gratitude isn't just a spiritual practice; it's brain training. If you train your mind to look for frustrations, you'll always find them. If you train it to look for blessings, you'll find those too. Gratitude doesn't change what's "out there"—but it absolutely changes what you notice, what you dwell on, and ultimately, how you live.

Your life is already full of "Jeeps"—blessings, opportunities, and reasons to be thankful. The question is: What are you looking for—problems or possibilities, complaints or gratitude?

"Praise the Lord, my soul,
and forget not all his benefits."
—Psalm 103:2

A Wider Lens

Tracy and I have been blessed to visit different parts of the world—places where people live with far less than we do. Earlier this year, we traveled to Costa Rica, a country known for its beaches, rainforests, and friendly people. Of course, we enjoyed the scenery and the food, but what I brought home was something even greater: a wider lens.

One morning, we played pickleball, then spent the afternoon exploring—hiking to the Llanos de Cortez Waterfall, sampling rich local coffee, and learning how chocolate is made. Throughout the day, we passed families whose homes were small, possessions few, and yet whose spirits seemed full.

I remember watching a group of kids kicking around a battered soccer ball with the biggest smiles on their faces. They didn't have the latest gadgets, or fancy playgrounds, but they had joy. And that joy was contagious.

It reminded me how easy it is to let small inconveniences steal our peace—a delayed flight, long lines at the grocery store, or waiting for someone to reply to an email. Gratitude isn't measured by possessions; it's shaped by perspective. In Costa Rica, families who had little in the way of material possessions, were still overflowing with gratitude for life's simple gifts: a shared meal, a safe place to sleep, or a game of soccer with friends.

Gratitude has a way of opening our eyes to what's already there, expanding our perspective and helping us notice blessings we might otherwise overlook. That's what happened to me in Costa Rica: my lens widened. Gratitude didn't just change what I saw; it changed *how* I saw.

Scripture points us in the same direction. Jesus said in Luke 12:15, *"Life does not consist in an abundance of possessions."* G.K. Chesterton put it this way: *"I would maintain that thanks are the highest form of thought, and that gratitude is happiness doubled by wonder."* Gratitude reframes our lives, showing us that joy isn't in what we accumulate, but in how deeply we appreciate.

Travel has a way of stripping away our blinders. But the truth is we don't need a passport to learn this lesson. Gratitude is available wherever we are.

Try stepping into your own life as if you were a visitor seeing it for the first time. What ordinary blessings would stand out, if you weren't used to them? A fresh perspective may be the very key to joy—right where you are.

"In the middle of every difficulty
lies opportunity."
—Albert Einstein

El Camino de Santiago

In June of 2025, I stepped out of my comfort zone and began a 500-mile pilgrimage across Spain—from St. Jean-Pied-de-Port to Santiago de Compostela. For 35 days, I traded convenience for simplicity: walking, praying, and paying attention. It was harder than I'd imagined—both physically and emotionally. By the end, I'd logged 1,177,183 steps, battling many moments of self-doubt that told me it was too hard.

During my walk, along with *I'm Gonna Be (500 Miles)* by The Proclaimers, I often found myself humming: "Now I've heard there was a secret chord that David played, and it pleased the Lord..." That "secret chord" wasn't about music theory. It was about David's heart. Despite his failures and brokenness, he had an unshakable devotion to God. He knew how to pour out praise, even from a place of struggle. That's what pleased the Lord.

So I began to thank God—out loud—for sore feet, for the hot sun, for the ache of the journey. I thanked Him for the losses that shaped me, the redirections that humbled me, and the grace that carried me through. Slowly, gratitude shifted my perspective. It didn't change my circumstances. It changed me.

Along the way, there was also incredible beauty: ever-changing landscapes, kind people, shared meals with pilgrims (who quickly became friends), and small but powerful reminders of God's presence. Grace showed up in the most ordinary places—a quiet village street, a blessing at evening mass, or the welcome from Benedictine monks.

On my third day, walking from Zubiri to Pamplona, I slowed down and walked with David, a fellow pilgrim living with Multiple sclerosis (MS). For over two hours, he shared his story and perspective on life. At one point, he quoted Ray Wylie Hubbard: *"The days that I keep my gratitude higher than my expectations, I have very good days."* Those words stuck with me. In that space between pain and grace, I realized that the Camino teaches every pilgrim the same prayer: gratitude.

Brother David Steindl-Rast once said, *"The root of joy is gratefulness… It is not joy that makes us grateful; it is gratitude that makes us joyful."* On the Camino, I found this to be true. Gratitude didn't come from everything going smoothly—it came from noticing simple gifts: a bed to sleep in, a hot meal, or just the strength to take another step. Gratitude opened the door to joy, even in hardship.

The walk reminded me that thankfulness is less about what we *feel* and more about what we *focus on*. When my eyes were fixed on the pain, that's all I could see. But when I lifted my head and noticed the beauty around me—the mountains in the distance, the kindness of a fellow pilgrim, the crunch of the path below my feet—blessings were everywhere.

Research backs this up. Scientists have found that gratitude reduces stress, improves mood, and even helps the body recover. I experienced this firsthand. When I focused on gratitude, instead of blisters or fatigue, the miles felt lighter.

Scripture says it this way: *"This is the day that the Lord has made; let us rejoice and be glad in it"* (Psalm 118:24). This verse became my rhythm. Every step was an invitation to rejoice—not after the struggle had ended, but right in the middle of it.

The Camino wasn't just a path across Spain; it was a reminder that gratitude is always available. We don't need to walk 500 miles to learn this lesson. Wherever we are—in our kitchen, our workplace, or sitting at the table with family—we can choose gratitude. It may not change the difficulty of the journey, but it will change how we walk through it. Gratitude doesn't wait for perfect conditions. It meets us with our feet sore, during long days, and in ordinary moments.

What small gift can you notice—and give thanks for—right where you are today?

"No winter lasts forever;
no spring skips its turn."
—Hal Borland

Forever Green

Every winter, the trees in my yard look dead. With their leaves gone, branches bare, they can look a little depressing. If you didn't know better, you might think they'd given up. But here's the truth: they're not dead at all. They're growing—just not in ways we can see. While the branches look barren, the roots are busy digging deeper, storing up strength for spring.

Gratitude works the same way in our lives. Sometimes we go through "winter seasons"—times that feel cold, quiet, and lifeless. Maybe it's waiting on test results, facing rejection at work, or navigating your way through a long stretch of setbacks. From the outside, nothing good looks like it's happening. But, just like the bamboo tree from the *Purposeful* chapter, underground, in the hidden places of our soul, God is still at work. Gratitude is what helps those roots stretch even deeper.

I lived through one of those winters myself. For years, I'd poured time and energy into my work. On the surface, everything looked fine—we had clients, revenue, and a growing team. But, underneath it all, I was burning out. Deep down, I kept wondering, *Is this really success? There has to be something more.* It became a long season of showing up, doing the work, and waiting for clarity. At times it felt barren, like nothing was moving forward. But looking back, I can see those years weren't wasted. They were a season of unseen growth, where God was shaping in me the resilience, skills, and perspective I would need for what came next.

And then came spring. When I finally stepped out of that chapter, new opportunities began to bloom—opportunities to speak, to write, and to do the work I truly felt called to do. The roots that had been stretching deep in "winter" made it possible for me to thrive in a new season. Without that unseen preparation, I wouldn't have been ready.

I'll admit, I've always preferred spring and summer. Springtime in Texas easily beats the cold winters I grew up with in Chicago. But winter has its purpose. The trees remind me that growth isn't always about what's visible; sometimes it's about what God is quietly building beneath the surface.

Gratitude in these winter seasons doesn't come naturally—it takes effort; it anchors us. It teaches us to pray, *"Lord, I trust You, even when I can't see the fruit yet."*

Albert Camus once wrote, *"In the depth of winter, I finally learned that within me there lay an invincible summer."* That line captures what gratitude makes possible: an ability to hold onto hope and trust even in barren seasons.

Scripture paints the same picture in Jeremiah 17:7–8:

"Blessed is the one who trusts in the Lord, whose confidence is in him. They will be like a tree planted by the water that sends out its roots by the stream. It does not fear when heat comes; its leaves are always green. It has no worries in a year of drought and never fails to bear fruit."

Even in the drought, even in the winter, the roots are reaching, preparing for fruit we can't yet see.

Gratitude in the barren seasons isn't about celebrating what's happening around us; it's about trusting what God is doing within us. It's believing that today's bare branches will lead to tomorrow's blossoms.

The next time life feels like winter—cold, quiet, and stripped bare—remember the unseen work happening underground. Gratitude in these moments deepens your roots, preparing you for the spring that's coming.

"Gratitude unlocks the fullness of life.
It turns what we have into enough, and more."
—Melody Beattie

Runner's High

There's a euphoric feeling that distance runners describe—known as the *runner's high*. Scientists say it comes from a surge of endorphins and endocannabinoids in the brain, producing a sense of calm, well-being, and even joy, after pushing through the pain. I'll be honest—I've never experienced this myself. After having both hips replaced in 2010, my doctor told me to only run if I was being chased by a bear.

Here's the good news: you don't have to be a marathoner

to experience something very similar. Gratitude produces its own kind of "runner's high." Neuroscientists have found that practicing gratitude activates the brain's reward pathways, triggering the release of dopamine and serotonin—the very chemicals that regulate mood, motivation, and happiness. At the University of California, Berkeley, scientists discovered that gratitude increases activity in the medial prefrontal cortex—the area of the brain that helps us make decisions and exercise self-control. The National Institutes of Health found that gratitude also activates the hypothalamus, the part of the brain that regulates stress, sleep, and even metabolism. In other words, gratitude doesn't just lift your mood—it strengthens your clarity, calms your body, and sustains your health. Put simply: gratitude is good for your brain, your body, and your soul.

Think about it: runners push through fatigue until a wave of endorphins gives them a second wind. Gratitude works the same way. When we push past complaining, self-pity, and comparison, we break through into a lighter, freer state of mind. Gratitude literally rewires the brain through a process called neuroplasticity—repeated thoughts strengthen neural pathways. The more we practice thankfulness, the easier it becomes for our minds to default to joy instead of negativity.

Gratitude is more than a mood boost—it's God's prescription for endurance.

And here's the best part: unlike running, gratitude doesn't require athletic ability. All of us can access its benefits. We can "train" our minds by giving thanks in the small moments: for the cup of coffee in our hands, the breath in our lungs, the person sitting across the table. Over time, those moments build momentum. Gratitude becomes our second wind—our spiritual runner's high.

The next time life feels like a marathon and you're tempted to quit, pause and ask yourself:

What's one small thing I can be grateful for right now? That single act of thanks may not remove the challenge, but it can give you the strength to keep moving forward.

"Train your mind to see the good in everything.
Positivity is a choice.
The happiness of your life depends on
the quality of your thoughts."
—Marcus Aurelius

Three Good Things

At the end of almost every keynote I give, I like to leave the audience with something practical. Something that doesn't take a ton of time but can make a big impact. One of my favorite practices is called Three Good Things. It's as simple as it sounds: before you go to bed, write down three good things that happened that day. That's it.

Documenting three good things isn't the only way to practice gratitude. Over the years, I've tried different practices to help me live with a more thankful heart—and the best part is, none of them are complicated. The more we practice gratitude in small ways, the more naturally it rises up in the big moments.

Sounds almost too easy, right? But here's the deal—research is compelling. Dr. Sonja Lyubomirsky, professor at UC Riverside, along with Dr. Ken Sheldon at the University of Missouri, found that people who wrote down three good things every night experienced a 2% increase in happiness after just one week. That might not sound like much, but think of it like compounding interest. If you deposited $100 and earned 2% interest every 7 days, by the end of a month you'd have $108.24. By the end of a year, you'd have $280. That's almost triple your money—all from tiny, steady deposits quietly compounding over time. Gratitude works the same way. Small daily practices may not feel like much in the moment, but when stacked day after day, they grow into something powerful, transforming how we see the world and how we live in it.

And Lyubomirsky and Sheldon aren't the only ones. A study from Dr. Martin Seligman at the University of Pennsylvania asked participants to write down three good things each day for a week. Not only did their happiness go up immediately, but many reported lower depression levels that lasted for six months. Think about that: one simple habit, just a few minutes each night, can ripple into half a year of greater joy and peace of mind.

In my workshops, I call this practice "Shine a Light on What is Right." TEDx speaker Anne Grady asks a similar question: "*What's right, right now?*" That shift in focus is what matters. Our brains are wired to notice problems and threats, more than blessings. Three Good Things flips the script. It forces us to scan for what's working, what's good, what's worth remembering. And the more we look for it, the more of it we'll see.

The trick is to be specific. "I'm thankful for my family" is nice, but "I'm thankful for Tracy making me laugh during our movie tonight" has weight. Specificity gives gratitude roots. It trains the brain to notice details, not just generalities.

Here are a few prompts that might help spark your list:

❧ What's one moment today that made you smile or laugh?

- What's one small win or step forward you had today?
- What's one simple gift—a meal, a hug, a quiet moment—that you're glad you didn't miss?
- Who encouraged you, supported you, or reminded you that you matter?
- Where did you catch a glimpse of God's goodness today?

You don't need a fancy journal. A scrap of paper, a note on your phone, or even saying them out loud at the dinner table, works. The point isn't *how* you do it—it's *that* you do it.

Gratitude practiced daily has a compounding effect. Over time, it shifts our perspective, rewires our brains, and deepens our joy. Scripture puts it this way: *"Every good and perfect gift is from above, coming down from the Father of the heavenly lights"* (James 1:17).

Every day is filled with gifts—big and small—if we'll only notice them. The question is: Will we start tonight? Will we shine a light on what is right, right now?

Noticing the good can rewire our brains, open our eyes, and even carry us through difficult and discouraging seasons. Writing down three good things at the end of the day is just one tool—a simple practice with big impact.

"Now is no time to think of what you do not have.
Think of what you can do with what there is."
– Ernest Hemingway

Gratitude Toolkit

Over the years, I've tried different practices to help me live with a more thankful heart—and the best part is, none of them are complicated. The more we practice gratitude in small ways, the more naturally it will rise up in the big moments.

In fact, researchers at Indiana University used brain scans to show that people who practiced simple gratitude exercises not only felt happier in the moment, but their brains actually rewired themselves to keep gratitude flowing long after the study ended. Small steps, repeated often, compound into something powerful. With that in mind, here are some practical gratitude tools that have made a big difference in my life—I believe they can do the same for you.

Gratitude Journal

I'll be honest—I don't always remember what I had for lunch yesterday, but I can tell you about something good that happened last week—because I wrote it down. That's the power of a gratitude journal: it locks in what our minds tend to skip past.

Why It Works: Writing turns fleeting moments into lasting memory. A UC Davis study by Dr. Robert Emmons found that people who kept weekly gratitude journals exercised more, reported fewer physical symptoms, and felt better about their lives overall. Other studies show that putting blessings into words actually rewires the brain to notice more positives over time. Writing doesn't just record gratitude—it multiplies it.

How I Use It: After my mom passed away, my dad was really struggling. An exercise that helped him was documenting three things first thing in the morning that he was grateful for or looking forward to, and three things in the evening that he'd learned or was thankful for. It wasn't complicated, but it gave him something steady to hold onto when everything else felt unsteady. Over time, it shifted his focus from what he'd lost to what he still had.

Gratitude doesn't erase grief, but it can soften its edges. By beginning and ending our days with thankfulness, we create bookends of perspective—reminders that, even in loss, God's mercies are new every morning (Lamentations 3:22–23). This practice spilled over into my own rhythm. Some days it's three big things; other days it's as small as a hot cup of coffee that really hit the spot. I even add a line to thank myself for something I did well. Gratitude toward others matters, but self-kindness matters just as much.

<u>My Action Plan (MAP):</u> Start tonight. Before going to bed, write down three things you're grateful for. Keep it simple. Over time, you'll start to notice more good in the moment because your brain is looking for it.

Gratitude Jar

At first glance, a jar filled with scraps of paper might not look impressive. But open one at the end of the year, and it transforms into a time capsule of thankfulness.

<u>Why It Works:</u> The jar makes gratitude visible. Each slip of paper is proof that blessings are all around us, even on days when we can't see them clearly. Psychologists call this *savoring*—the practice of reliving a good memory to strengthen its positive impact. In fact, research shows that recalling positive experiences boosts happiness almost as much as living them the first time. Proverbs 3:3 says, "*Write them on the tablet of your heart.*" In this case, I write them on scraps of paper and toss them in a jar.

How I Use It: At the beginning of the year, Tracy bought jars for me, Kip, and Kait. She gave us cut up slips of colored paper. Each day I write something I'm grateful for: a text from a friend, a big win on the pickleball court, a great dinner with Tracy, or a quiet day in my office, writing. They don't have to be profound; they just have to be real. At the end of the year, I pour them out and read them aloud—a highlight reel of joy that no sports network could rival.

My Action Plan (MAP): Find a jar. Put it somewhere you'll see it often. Each day, jot down one moment of gratitude. By the year's end, you'll hold in your hands a collection of blessings—a reminder that even ordinary days are filled with extraordinary gifts.

Gratitude Walk

Sometimes the best gratitude list isn't written—it's walked. Henry David Thoreau said, *"An early-morning walk is a blessing for the whole day."* Our feet become the pen, the trail our paper. Each step writes gratitude into our story. Step by step, thankfulness has a way of moving from something we think about to something we embody. Unlike a journal, where gratitude is captured in ink, a gratitude walk engraves it into our memory and lifts our mood.

Why It Works: Walking lowers stress, boosts circulation, and clears the mind. When you add gratitude to the rhythm of each step, the benefits multiply. Research from Barbara Fredrickson shows that positive emotions like thankfulness "broaden and build" our awareness, helping us notice beauty and opportunities we would otherwise miss. Psalm 119:45 puts it this way: *"I will walk about in freedom, for I have sought out your precepts."* Walking with gratitude is freedom in motion—freedom from stress, self-focus, and negativity.

How I Use It: When I walk on the trails in our neighborhood, I silently thank God for small gifts I notice—sunlight through the trees, a kind neighbor's wave, the peaceful sound of the San Gabriel River. Sometimes, I make it a game: A–Z gratitude. "A" for acorns scattered under oak trees, "B" for butterflies dancing around flowerbeds, "C" for cactus thriving in the sun. I've even layered in what I call *gratitude breaths*—inhale thanks, exhale thanks. Each step becomes a prayer, each breath an act of worship.

My Action Plan (MAP): Take a gratitude walk this week. Try the A–Z gratitude game, breathe prayers of thanks with each step, or simply notice one thing you've overlooked before. Gratitude doesn't just change your pace—it changes your perspective.

Naikan Reflection

This practice began in Japan in the 1940s with a man named Ishin Yoshimoto, a devout Buddhist who developed Naikan (which means "looking inside") as a spiritual discipline. Over time, it spread beyond temples and counseling centers into schools, prisons, and even business settings—anywhere people needed to grow in self-awareness and compassion.

Why It Works: Naikan is less about listing things and more about changing perspective. Instead of asking, *What do I want?* Naikan asks, *What have I already received?* It's a shift that moves us from scarcity to abundance, and from complaint to compassion. Naikan is built on three simple but searching questions:

1. What have I received?
2. What have I given?
3. What difficulties have I caused?

These questions pull us out of self-centeredness. Instead of focusing on what's missing, we notice what's already been provided—often far more than we realize. Research in positive psychology shows that reflecting on how others contribute to our well-being, increases empathy and strengthens relationships. Philippians 2:4 echoes this call: *"Look not only to your own interests, but also to the interests of others."* Gratitude deepens, when we see how interconnected our lives really are.

<u>How I Use It:</u> Some nights I'll journal my answers, other times I pray through them. It keeps me grounded, especially on the days when I'm tempted to only see what went wrong. Naming what I've received, reminds me of God's provision. Naming what I've given, calls me to keep showing up. Naming the difficulties I've caused, humbles me, reminding me that gratitude isn't just about blessings—it's about responsibility. Gratitude isn't just about things; it's about the people who shape our lives, the grace that covers us, and the awareness to see both.

<u>My Action Plan (MAP):</u> This week, sit with these three questions. Write out your answers—don't overthink, don't judge, just notice. Let it stretch your perspective. Gratitude grows not just by counting blessings, but by seeing the bigger story of how God weaves us into one another's lives.

Flip the Script

Life will hand you detours, delays, and disappointments. Gratitude doesn't erase them, but it can reframe them. This practice is sometimes called *cognitive reframing*—learning to see the same situation through a different, more hopeful lens.

Why It Works: When we change the lens, we choose to shift our attention from frustration to possibility. Psychologists note that reframing reduces stress, improves resilience, and helps us respond with flexibility, rather than frustration. In other words, it doesn't deny reality; it asks, *What's right, right now?* Even in difficulty, there is almost always some hidden grace—a lesson learned, a relationship strengthened, or simply a moment of slowing down. Scripture echoes this truth: *"In all things God works for the good of those who love him"* (Romans 8:28). Gratitude helps us find the good that God is weaving, even when it's hidden.

How I Use It: Travel delays tend to make me crazy. I'm grumpy at the airport, I'm constantly watching the clock, and I get more and more frustrated by the minute. Now, I try to flip the script. An extra hour gives me time to read, unplug, or get in my daily 10,000 steps. When work stress piles up, instead of only focusing on the pressure, I ask, *What's the hidden gift here?* Sometimes it's perspective. Sometimes it's patience. Sometimes it's just a funny story to tell later. Gratitude may not change the situation, but it always changes how I walk through it.

My Action Plan (MAP): Next time you face frustration, stop and flip it. Write down one thing that could be good in disguise. Over time, you'll train your brain to default to thankfulness, even when life doesn't go according to plan.

Thank-You Cards

Emails are fine. Texts are quick. But a handwritten note? That sticks. William Arthur Ward says, *"Feeling gratitude and not expressing it is like wrapping a present and not giving it."* In a world that runs on instant messages and emojis, the effort of picking up a pen, slowing down, and writing words of gratitude, carries a weight that digital communication just can't replicate.

Why It Works: Research from the University of Chicago found that people consistently underestimate how meaningful a handwritten note of gratitude is to the recipient. The study showed that even short, simple notes deeply touched people—often far more than the sender expected. And the impact lasts: recipients reported feeling uplifted for weeks, long after the envelope was opened. Proverbs 16:24 says, *"Gracious words are a honeycomb, sweet to the soul and healing to the bones."* A thank-you card is a tangible way to deliver those sweet words.

How I Use It: I've done "30 thank-you cards in 30 days"—for clients, friends, people I've met at conferences—each card was a chance to pause and reflect on the influence someone had on my life. The responses I got back were moving. More than once, I've been told that a person kept the card, sometimes tucked in a drawer or pinned to a bulletin board. Nobody keeps a text message on the fridge, but a handwritten note often becomes a keepsake.

My Action Plan (MAP): Pick one person this week. Write them a handwritten note of thanks. Put it in the mail. Don't worry about using perfect words—sincerity matters more than eloquence.

Gratitude in Action

Gratitude doesn't just live in journals or jars—it comes alive when we put it into motion. Oscar Wilde says, *"The smallest act of kindness is worth more than the grandest intention."* True thankfulness doesn't stop at feeling blessed; it overflows into how we treat others. Gratitude in action transforms not just our outlook, but the world around us.

Why It Works: Small acts of kindness are gratitude expressed outwardly. Research from Emory University found that helping others activates the brain's reward centers, releasing dopamine and oxytocin—the same "feel-good" chemicals that flood our brains when *receiving* gratitude. In other words, when you show kindness, you don't just lift someone else's spirit—you also lift your own.

Rick Rigsby, in his book *Lessons from a Third Grade Dropout*, challenges readers to put gratitude in motion through several simple practices: say "thank you", open doors for others, smile at strangers, listen more than you talk, or help those who can't repay you. These are simple practices, but they are contagious.

How I Use It: There have been weeks where I've tried to intentionally choose one of Rick's challenges each day—like letting someone go ahead of me in line, offering words of encouragement, or talking less about myself and listening more. It's amazing how quickly your perspective shifts when gratitude becomes something you do, not just something you feel. Those small acts remind me that gratitude is meant to ripple outward, blessing others the same way I've been blessed.

My Action Plan (MAP): Pick one act of kindness from Rick's list each day, for the next week. At the end of the week, reflect on how it changed your outlook—and how it might've changed someone else's day.

Gratitude Groups

Some things are best shared—and gratitude is at the top of the list. While personal journaling and reflection build a strong foundation, gratitude multiplies when it's spoken aloud and experienced together. It has a way of drawing people closer, softening edges, and creating an atmosphere where joy is easier to find.

Why It Works: Speaking about gratitude in a group helps build connection and strengthens bonds. Research shows that collective gratitude practices can improve team morale, deepen friendships, and increase family closeness. In one study, couples who regularly expressed gratitude to one another reported stronger relationships and greater resilience during conflict. Gratitude has a social dimension—it's not just felt, it's shared. Scripture affirms this truth: *"For where two or three gather in my name, there am I with them"* (Matthew 18:20). Gratitude gathers us, and God meets us there.

How I Use It: Some families I know go around the dinner table naming one thing they're grateful for, and it changes the tone of the meal. On corporate teams, I've seen people share gratitude at the start of meetings, and the whole room shifts. Even volunteering with others can become a form of thankfulness—giving thanks by giving back. And, when Tracy and I share gratitude with one another, it builds intimacy and perspective that nothing else can.

My Action Plan (MAP): Add a gratitude round to your next meal, meeting, or gathering. Keep it simple—one sentence each. Watch how quickly the atmosphere changes when thankfulness is spoken into the room.

The Roman philosopher Cicero once said, *"Gratitude is not only the greatest of virtues, but the parent of all the others."* Gratitude reshapes how we see the world, and how we see the world reshapes how we live in it. These practices give us a lens to see God's fingerprints in every part of our story.

"But someone will say, "You have faith; I have deeds."
Show me your faith without deeds,
and I will show you my faith by my deeds."
—James 2:18

From Thankful to Mindful

Writing about living with purpose, joy, prayer, and thankfulness isn't meant to stay words on a page—it's meant to become the way you live. Gratitude isn't just something you feel; it's something you practice until it shapes your words, your choices, and your relationships.

The first four chapters are about knowing what matters, this final chapter is about putting it into motion.

Mindfulness is more than slowing down or being present in the moment—it's about living intentionally, with your heart and mind anchored in the truths you've learned. It's choosing to notice God's hand in your life, align your actions with your values, and make space for the things that truly matter.

In this final chapter, we'll explore how to take what you've learned—purpose, joy, prayer, and thankfulness—and turn it into daily rhythms that bring steadiness to your soul, clarity to your days, and a deeper awareness of God at work all around you.

Mindful

ADJECTIVE:
Conscious or aware of something;
attentive to the present moment,
thoughts, or surroundings.

Daisaku Ikeda

"Everything begins with the resolve to take the first step.
From that action, wisdom arises, and change begins.
Without action, nothing changes."

Ephesians 5:15–16

"Be very careful, then, how you live
—not as unwise but as wise,
making the most of every opportunity,
because the days are evil."

Pancake Problems

A few weekends ago, I was making pancakes—a special treat for me and Tracy—since we usually try to start the day a little healthier. (Let's be honest, egg whites and spinach don't exactly scream "weekend celebration.")

Now, anyone who's ever made pancakes knows the struggle of the first pancake. It's either undercooked in the middle, burnt around the edges, too flat, too thick—or somehow all of the above. It's practically a universal truth in the kitchen: the first pancake rarely turns out perfect.

But here's the thing—that first pancake isn't a failure. It's feedback. It's a teacher. As the saying goes: FAIL just means *'First Attempt In Learning.'*

When you're trying something new—whether it's writing your first draft of a book, learning pickleball, or giving a keynote presentation—it's easy to feel discouraged, if it doesn't go smoothly. But, just like making pancakes, the first attempt is essential. It shows you how the batter spreads, how the pan heats, how long to wait before flipping. You adjust, you tweak, you learn. And before long, those golden, fluffy pancakes are stacking up beautifully.

Psychologists call this the *"beginner's effect."* The first attempt at anything can be clumsy because our brains are busy processing dozens of new variables at once. The more we repeat, the more automatic it becomes. (Think about tying your shoes, riding a bike, or doing your job—all of them started with awkward first tries.)

Even Thomas Edison understood this principle. When asked about the thousands of failed attempts to invent the light bulb, he replied: *"I have not failed. I've just found 10,000 ways that won't work."*

Scripture says it another way: *"Do not despise these small beginnings, for the Lord rejoices to see the work begin"* (Zechariah 4:10). God delights not only in the finished product, but also in our willingness to take that imperfect first step.

So maybe your first pancake isn't pretty. Maybe your first swing in pickleball goes straight into the net. Maybe your first big presentation has you gripping the podium with sweaty palms. That's okay. Every "first pancake" is part of the recipe for progress.

What matters is this: Don't give up. Flip it. Learn from it. Adjust. And move on to the next one. Progress always starts messy—but the good stuff usually shows up when you keep going.

"All things are difficult
before they are easy."
—Thomas Fuller

Guitar Hero

When Kip received Guitar Hero for Christmas, he was thrilled. If you've never seen it, it's a video game where you hold a plastic guitar with colored buttons instead of strings and try to hit those buttons as the notes race down your TV screen. Think karaoke meets rock concert—in your living room.

Kip loves video games, so this one was an instant hit. Within weeks, he was playing on expert level and putting on living-room concerts that were surprisingly entertaining. Naturally, this sparked a new dream: he wanted to be a rock star. He even started saving for a real guitar.

Tracy and I have always tried to support our kids, so we paid for lessons to help him along. But here's where things took a turn. Two weeks into guitar lessons, he realized something painful: real guitars don't come with colored buttons, cheat codes, or a "restart song" option. Suddenly, the instant success he felt with the video game wasn't there. He was discouraged and ready to quit.

I decided to share one of my favorite life lessons: *"Everything is difficult, until it isn't."* Kip looked at me. "Dad, is that from one of your workshops?"

I laughed and said *yes*. Then I explained that when you start something new, it can feel awkward, hard, and maybe even impossible. But the more you practice, the easier it becomes. Eventually, the thing that once felt overwhelming becomes second nature.

Psychologists call this the *competence curve*. At first, you're consciously incompetent (you know you're bad at it). Then, with repetition, you move to conscious competence (you can do it, but you have to think about it). Finally, with enough practice, you reach unconscious competence—it's automatic. Whether it's starting a new job, learning a language, or giving your first big presentation, everything follows this curve.

John Maxwell puts it this way: *"You don't get good at something by waiting to feel good. You get good by working through the awkward stage."*

Scripture reinforces the same truth. Hebrews 12:11 reminds us: *"No discipline seems pleasant at the time, but painful. Later on, however, it produces a harvest of righteousness and peace for those who have been trained by it."* In other words, growth feels hard at first, but it pays off if we stick with it.

When you're learning something new, it will almost always feel harder than you expected. The difference between "hard" and "habit" is simply repetition plus time. That's not failure—it's training. Stick with it long enough, and the impossible will one day feel automatic. Remember: *everything is difficult, until it isn't.*

\|/

"Whatever you want to do,
if you want to be great at it,
you have to love it and
be able to make sacrifices for it."
—Dr. Maya Angelou

The Karate Kid

Whether you saw the original *The Karate Kid* in 1984 (I was in high school then), or the remake years later, you probably remember the scene where young Daniel asks Mr. Miyagi to teach him karate. Mr. Miyagi agrees—but only on one condition: Daniel must submit completely to his instruction and never question his methods.

Daniel shows up eager to learn punches, kicks, and secret karate moves. Instead, Mr. Miyagi assigns him three chores. Do you remember what they were?

First came the cars—wash and wax. And of course, the famous line: "Wax on, wax off." Next was painting the fence—up and down, up and down. Finally, scrubbing the deck with a precise circular motion.

Daniel spends days completing these tasks, growing more frustrated by the minute. Finally, he bursts: "I thought you were going to teach me karate! All you've done is make me do your chores!"

Mr. Miyagi's face hardens. "I have been teaching you karate! Defend yourself!" Suddenly, he throws a punch. Daniel instinctively blocks with the "paint the fence" motion. A second strike is deflected with "scrub the deck." A kick is stopped with "wax on, wax off." Only then does Daniel realize what his teacher had known all along: true skill comes from faithfully repeating the correct, but seemingly mundane, actions.

This lesson isn't just about karate. It's about life. The small, ordinary disciplines—daily gratitude, short prayers, choosing kindness, focusing on what matters—don't always look impressive, but they quietly shapestrength, character, and wisdom over time. As Darren Hardy once said: *"Small, seemingly insignificant steps completed consistently over time will create a radical difference."*

And scripture reminds us: *"Whoever can be trusted with very little can also be trusted with much"* (Luke 16:10). God often uses the small, repeated actions of faithfulness to prepare us for greater responsibility.

The Karate Kid reminds us that growth doesn't come from shortcuts, but from consistent practice of the right habits. Joy, prayer, and thankfulness don't become second nature overnight—they're formed through small, steady repetitions. Keep showing up. Keep practicing. Over time, those ordinary motions will become extraordinary strength.

"You are valuable simply because you exist.
Not because of what you do or what you have done,
but simply because you are."
—Max Lucado

$8 Bottle of Water

A few years back, I went on a baseball tour with my mom and dad. It was one of those trips you don't forget—ballpark hot dogs, nachos, big laughs, wonderful memories. At Wrigley Field in Chicago (my all-time favorite ballpark), I was feeling dehydrated and went to grab a bottle of water. That's when I nearly fell over. The price tag? Eight dollars. Eight bucks... for water. Back home, that same bottle costs about ten cents at the grocery store. Same brand. Same water. What changed? The setting.

Here's the lesson: your value *doesn't* change—but how it's recognized often depends on where you are and how you're being used. There's a well-known quote that captures this truth perfectly: "If you judge a fish by its ability to climb a tree, it will live its whole life believing that it is stupid."

Sometimes we undervalue ourselves—thinking we're worth about ten cents. Other times, we buy into the "ballpark price tag," letting the world's temporary measures define us. But God says our worth isn't based on where we're standing—it's based on who we are in Him.

Paul reminds us in 1 Corinthians 12:7: *"Now to each one the manifestation of the Spirit is given for the common good."* We've all been given spiritual gifts. Their true value isn't in keeping them on the shelf—it's in using and developing them for God's purposes.

I thought about this, again, when I read that at the Paul "Bear" Bryant Museum at the University of Alabama, tour guides share that Coach Bryant carried a prayer in his wallet and often pulled it out to read to players and friends—a prayer commonly attributed to William Arthur Ward:

> "This is the beginning of a new day. God has given me this day to use as I will. I can waste it or use it for good. What I do today is very important because I am exchanging a day of my life for it. When tomorrow comes, this day will be gone forever, leaving something in its place I have traded for it. I want it to be gain, not loss—good, not evil; success, not failure—in order that I shall not forget the price I paid for it."

This prayer is a powerful reminder: your time, your gifts, your very life—all has immense value. Don't undervalue what God has placed in you. Don't settle for less than the life He designed you to live.

Your worth isn't determined by where you are or what others see—it's determined by the God who made you. He's given you gifts, talents, and opportunities, and each day is a chance to invest them for something eternal. The question isn't how much you're worth—it's how you'll use what you've been given today.

"Dig deep within yourself,
for there is a fountain of goodness ever ready to flow
if you keep digging."
—***Marcus Aurelius***

Instant Millionaire

Like so many ranchers who would soon be devastated by the Great Depression, Ira and Ann Yates were already struggling to survive in the 1920s, their family living on government relief. They owned a sheep ranch with more than 20,000 acres in West Texas, and were in danger of losing it because they couldn't pay the mortgage.

Then, in 1926, a crew from Transcontinental Oil (now part of Marathon Oil) surveyed the land and suggested there might be oil beneath the surface. Desperate, Yates signed a lease to let them drill. At 1,115 feet, they struck a massive gusher—the first well alone produced 80,000 barrels a day. Successive wells produced more than double that. Even thirty years later, one well was still capable of producing 125,000 barrels a day. To date, the Yates field has produced over a billion barrels—and nearly a century later, it's still pumping oil.

Here's the irony: Ira Yates was sitting on unimaginable wealth, but he lived the life of a poor rancher because he didn't know what was beneath his feet.

So here's the question I ask in my keynotes: Was Ira Yates an instant millionaire, or had he always been a millionaire? The lesson isn't about oil or money—it's about the treasure often hidden beneath the surface of our own lives.

We all have untapped potential—talents, dreams, resources, and gifts that may feel buried or unused. The call isn't to wait for someone else to discover them—it's to recognize and invest in what God has already placed inside you. Your worth isn't defined by circumstance, timing, or visibility. Some of your gifts may be dormant. Some may be just waiting for discovery. Tend to them faithfully, cultivate them patiently, and trust God's timing to bring them to the surface. One practical tool that helped me better understand and name my own strengths is the book *Strengths Finder 2.0* from Tom Rath.

As Paul wrote to Timothy: *"Fan into flame the gift of God, which is in you"* (2 Timothy 1:6). Your gifts are already there—they just need to be brought to the surface, sharpened, and set on fire.

"The two most powerful warriors
are patience and time."
– *Leo Tolstoy*

Big Things Take Time

I came across a story that's been shared for years, and I love the lesson it teaches.

An elephant and a dog became pregnant at the same time.

Three months later, the dog gave birth to six puppies. Six months later, she was pregnant again and gave birth to another litter. Nine months after that... yet another. The cycle continued.

Meanwhile, the elephant was still pregnant.

Eighteen months in, the dog couldn't take it anymore. "Are you sure you're pregnant?" she asked the elephant. "We got pregnant at the same time. I've had three litters of puppies, while you haven't given birth to anything. What's going on?"

The elephant replied, "What you don't understand is this: I'm not carrying a puppy—I'm carrying an elephant. I only give birth once every two years. But, when my baby hits the ground, the earth feels it. When it crosses the road, people stop and watch. What I'm carrying is mighty and worth the wait."

The moral is simple: Don't compare your timeline with someone else's. Puppies are wonderful, so are elephants, but elephants take more time. The fact that your dream, gift, or calling hasn't "shown up" yet doesn't mean it's not real—it may just mean something bigger than you imagined is coming.

Author Mel Robbins puts it this way: *"Stop comparing yourself to others. It's a recipe for unhappiness. Your journey is unique, and so is your timing."* The Apostle Paul echoes that warning in 2 Corinthians 10:12: *"When they measure themselves by themselves and compare themselves with themselves, they are not wise."*

Comparison is a trap—it steals your joy and blinds you to the unique life God has set before you. God's timing isn't about keeping up with anyone else's pace. It's about preparing you for what He's already planted inside you.

I will often share this advice with others (I need it for myself too.): *Do You!* If you compare your calling to someone else's, you'll often feel like you're behind. But, if you stay faithful to the season you're in, your time *will* come—and when it does, people will take notice. Don't measure your progress against someone else's timeline. Trust God's timing. Be patient with your journey. Remember—the world doesn't stop for every puppy, but when the elephant arrives, everyone notices.

This story is so powerful it's stayed with me—and it may even shape the title of my next book: *Do You.* Because the best thing you can do isn't trying to match someone else's pace—it's faithfully living the unique race God designed for you.

> "Success seems to be connected to action.
> Successful people keep moving.
> They make mistakes, but they don't quit."
> —***Conrad Hilton***

God Will Save Me

I first heard this story at church years ago, and it's worth retelling here.

Farmer Brown was a devoted believer. When the Emergency Broadcast System declared a state of emergency and urged everyone to evacuate due to rising floodwaters, Farmer Brown refused to leave. "I'm not worried," he said. "I've prayed, and I'm trusting that God will save me."

As the water rose and covered his porch, a neighbor paddled up in a small boat.

"Hop in —I'll take you to safety!"

But Farmer Brown waved him off. "No thanks. God's got this. He's going to rescue me."

A few hours later, the water crept up to the second floor.

A rescue team in a larger boat called out, "Come with us—this may be your last chance!"

Still, Farmer Brown refused. "I'm not going anywhere. I'm waiting on the Lord."

Eventually, he had to climb onto the roof.

A helicopter flew overhead and lowered a rope. The crew shouted, "Grab the rope—we've got you!"

But Farmer Brown stood firm. "God will save me," he yelled back.

Soon after, the floodwaters consumed the house—and Farmer Brown drowned.

When he got to heaven, he asked God, "Lord, I believed in You. I prayed. Why didn't You save me?"

And God said, "I sent you an emergency alert. I sent you two boats. I even sent a helicopter. What else were you looking for?"

Dr. Paul Berg puts it this way: *"Faith isn't just believing God can move, but really listening and being willing to move with Him."*

Faith means trusting God—but it also means paying attention and taking action. Sometimes, we expect a miracle and miss the help God is already sending through people, opportunities, or interruptions. Just because it doesn't look supernatural doesn't mean it isn't God.

James 2:17 says it this way: *"Faith by itself, if it is not accompanied by action, is dead."*

Prayer and trust are essential, but they're not replacements for obedience and action.

I often think of it like the automatic doors at the grocery store. They only open when you take a step forward. You can stand there waiting, but nothing happens until you move.

Faith works the same way. Prayer isn't meant to replace action—it's meant to *precede* it. We pray, we trust, and then we move.

Step toward the open door, grab the rope, climb into the boat. Sometimes the miracle isn't God doing it all for you—it's God giving you the nudge and the opportunity to take action.

Faith isn't passive—it's active trust. Don't sit on the roof waiting for a miracle only to miss the rescue God has already sent. Pray. Trust. Step forward. Remember... *the doors don't open until you move.*

"Pray as though everything depended on God.
Work as though everything depended on you."
—St. Ignatius of Loyola

Prayerful Action

Nehemiah was a Jewish exile serving as cupbearer to King Artaxerxes of Persia in the 5th century B.C.

A cupbearer was a high-ranking royal official whose primary duty was to serve wine to the king—ensuring its safety by tasting it first. It was a position of trust, influence, and proximity to power.

At first glance, Nehemiah's life seemed secure. But when he heard that the walls of Jerusalem—the city of his ancestors—were still in ruins nearly a century after the first return from exile, his heart broke. A city without walls was vulnerable to attack, shame, and instability.

The first thing Nehemiah did was pray. He wept, fasted, confessed the sins of his people, and pleaded for God's favor (Nehemiah 1). But he didn't stop there. Nehemiah turned prayer into action. He boldly asked the king for permission, protection, and resources to rebuild. With God's hand upon him, the king granted his request.

When Nehemiah arrived in Jerusalem, he got to work. He inspected the walls, rallied the people, and developed a plan. Even when enemies mocked, threatened, and tried to sabotage the project, Nehemiah pressed forward. Scripture records that the people "worked with all their heart" (Nehemiah 4:6), and remarkably, the wall was rebuilt in just 52 days (Nehemiah 6:15).

Nehemiah's story is one of prayerful action. He sought God's direction at every turn, yet he also rolled up his sleeves and worked. He prayed as if everything depended on God and acted as if everything depended on him.

It's a powerful reminder for us today: waiting on God doesn't mean doing nothing. Prayer and action are not opposites—they're partners. Nehemiah shows us that when faith is paired with courage, strategy, and obedience, God can use us to rebuild what is broken—in our lives, in our communities, and in our world.

Maybe God has placed a burden on your heart—a dream, a relationship that needs mending, a cause worth fighting for, or even a habit that needs breaking. Don't just pray for change. Pray, yes—but also roll up your sleeves. Send the text. Make the call. Sign up for the class. Start the conversation. Write the first page. Take the first step.

For me, this book is an example of this. I spent more than seven years thinking about it, praying about it, outlining it, and talking about it. But the thinking wasn't finishing the book. It wasn't until my walk on El Camino de Santiago that I got serious about seeing it through. That time of prayer and reflection clarified what mattered—and when I came home, I finally sat down and finished writing. Prayer prepared the way—but action completed the work.

Nehemiah reminds us that God doesn't just answer prayers through miracles in the sky—He often answers them through the faithful actions of His people. Pray like it all depends on God. Act like it all depends on you.

"Don't dwell on what went wrong.
Instead, focus on what to do next.
Spend your energies on moving forward
toward finding the answer."
—Denis Waitley

The Widowmaker

When Kait graduated from high school, she wanted to celebrate with something adventurous, so Tracy and I took her white-water rafting in Buena Vista, Colorado. We strapped on our helmets, tightened our life jackets, and listened to the instructions from our guide, Zach.

Before we pushed off, Zach gave us the plan. With over twenty years on the Arkansas River, he grinned and said, "Nothing to worry about." I believed him—until he introduced our first rapid: *The Widowmaker*.

Zach laid out our options.

- *Plan A:* "We go straight through the middle. Everyone paddles as hard as you can. If you give it everything, we'll punch right through."
- *Plan B:* "If we don't paddle hard enough or straight enough, the current will push us to the side into a swirling whirlpool. We won't flip, but we'll sit there watching other rafts pass us until we claw our way back out."
- *Plan C:* (the one I didn't love) "If we hit it wrong and topple, don't panic. Feet up, ride the current. I'll meet you downriver."

As the roar got louder and the boat drifted toward the white water, my grip tightened. And I realized: this rapid is life in a snapshot. Because in life, you really have the same three choices. You can face it head-on—digging in with courage and persistence and moving forward together. You can let the current push you aside—stuck in a whirlpool—watching others pass while you keep telling yourself you'll paddle "later". Or you can topple—get knocked under, then drift until you eventually find your way back (if you do at all).

You don't get to name the rapid—grief, fear, failure, or uncertainty—but you do get to choose your response. And the way through is always the same: paddle hard, don't quit in the middle, and listen to your Guide.

That day, we hit the Widowmaker head-on. Water splashed over us, the raft shook, and Kait screamed and laughed at the same time. We came out the other side soaked, shaking, and grinning. Scripture says it this way in Isaiah 43:2: *"When you pass through the waters, I will be with you."*

Life will hand you Widowmakers. Don't get stuck in the whirlpool. Don't surrender to the current. Paddle through. Choose Plan A: show up with courage, give it everything, and move forward with your people.

What rapid are you facing right now? What's one "paddle stroke" you can take today—the call, the meeting, the application, the apology? And most importantly, whose voice will you trust as your Guide? You won't always choose the waters—but you can always choose your response.

"A lot of life's problems can be solved
by getting up in the morning and going to work."
—Russ Boles

Be a Buffalo

Along the Colorado Front Range, storms sweep across the plains from the west. There's a well-known metaphor about cows and buffalo that's often used to describe how we respond to life's storms.

When cows sense a storm coming, they instinctively try to run away from it. They head east, in the opposite direction of the approaching thunder. But cows aren't fast. The storm eventually overtakes them, and because they keep moving with it, they stay in it longer, prolonging their fear, frustration, and exhaustion.

Buffalos respond differently. When a storm approaches, they turn and face it head-on. Instead of trying to avoid it, they charge directly into it. By doing so, they pass through it faster and minimize the time and suffering they spend in the storm.

That contrast paints a vivid picture of how *we* can handle life's challenges. We all face storms—illness, grief, financial strain, broken relationships, uncertainty about the future. Some of us try to outrun them, hoping they'll just disappear. But often, running only keeps us in the storm longer. Like the buffalo, the wiser way is to face the storm with courage, faith, and resolve.

Scripture reminds us of this truth: *"Be strong and courageous. Do not be afraid; do not be discouraged, for the Lord your God will be with you wherever you go."* (Joshua 1:9).

God doesn't promise a storm-free life, but He does promise His presence in the storm—and His strength when we face it.

So the next time storm clouds rise on your horizon, don't be the cow. Don't prolong the pain by trying to avoid what's ahead. Be the buffalo. Turn toward it. Step into it. Move through it with faith, knowing God is with you in the middle of it all.

What storm are you in right now? Are you running from it? Circling in it? Or charging through it?

What would it look like to stop running and face it head-on, with God's strength as your guide?

"Unless commitment is made,
there are only promises and hopes...
but no plans."
—Peter F. Drucker

Eggs and Ham

A few years back, I heard a story at our church's leadership retreat that's worth retelling.

A church was raising funds for a family who'd lost everything in a fire. Out in the barnyard, a hen and a pig overheard the appeal and wanted to help.

The hen spoke up first. "I know! Let's give them eggs and ham."

The pig frowned. "Easy for you to say. For you, that's just a contribution. For me, that's total commitment."

It's a lighthearted story, but the truth behind it hits close to home. In life—and especially in faith—we often face the same choice. Will we settle for contribution—giving what's convenient—or step into commitment, offering ourselves fully, even when it costs us something?

Leadership works the same way. Families thrive the same way. Teams succeed the same way. Real impact doesn't come from half-efforts; it comes from commitment. As Ken Blanchard once said: *"There's a difference between interest and commitment. When you're interested in something, you do it only when it's convenient. When you're committed, you accept no excuses—only results."*

Jesus put it even more directly in Luke 9:23: *"Whoever wants to be my disciple must deny themselves and take up their cross daily and follow me."*

Contribution is good, but commitment changes everything. In faith, in family, and in work, the question remains: Are you the hen—or the pig? Where are you just contributing, and where is God calling you to commit?

"Don't take shortcuts;
if I want to be true to my beliefs,
then shortcuts do not exist."
—DeVon Franklin

Build With Care

A friend once shared this story with me, and I've never forgotten it.

Chuck the carpenter was ready to retire.

He told his employer he was leaving the home-building business to enjoy a more relaxed life with his wife and extended family. He knew he'd miss the paycheck, but he was ready.

His employer was sorry to lose one of his best; he asked if Chuck would build just one more house—as a personal favor. Reluctantly, Chuck agreed.

It was obvious his heart wasn't in it. He cut corners. He used cheaper materials. He rushed through the work. It was a disappointing way to finish an otherwise strong career.

When the house was finished, the employer came for a final walk-through. At the end, he handed Chuck the keys and said, "This is your house. My gift to you."

Chuck was stunned. If he had known he was building his own house, he would have done everything differently. Now he had to live in the home he had built—shortcuts and all.

It's the same with our lives.

Each day, we're placing boards, hammering nails, and laying foundations with our choices, words, and habits. Too often, we get distracted or careless. We rush. We settle. We treat the day like it doesn't matter. But then one day, we look around and realize—we're living in the life we've been building all along.

At the end of the day, you are the carpenter. Whether you're building for one more year, one more season, or just one more day, build it with purpose and care. Paul reminds us in 1 Corinthians 3:10: *"Each one should build with care."*

Your life, today, is the result of yesterday's choices. And the choices you make today will shape the "house" you live in tomorrow. So build wisely—because you're the one who will be living there!

> "The shortest way to do many things
> is to only do one thing at a time."
> —***Mozart***

Keep Your Left Elbow Straight

I remember when Tracy gave me a gift card for a golf lesson at a place in Austin called Golf Smith. I was excited. The pro walked me through it all—how to grip the club, where to stand, how to follow through. Every moment felt useful.

After my lesson, armed with new knowledge, I took a bucket of balls to the range. But instead of improving, I got worse. Why? Because I was thinking about too many things at once. I was so focused on all the little corrections that I lost sight of simply hitting the ball. Frustrated, I eventually gave up golf altogether.

Fast forward a dozen years. I was driving Kip to his golf lesson at Teravista Golf Club. While he worked with his instructor, I stepped into the open bay next to him and hit a few shots—hoping time away might have magically fixed my game. But it hadn't. My shots still went everywhere except straight.

Kip's instructor noticed, walked over, watched my swing, and gave me just one tip: "Keep your left elbow straight." That was it. Just one thing. My shots weren't perfect, but they were straighter—straight enough for me to actually play a round with Kip.

That day I learned something important: sometimes less really is more. When I tried to fix everything, I got stuck. When I focused on one thing, I improved.

Life works the same way. We get overwhelmed by everything we think we need to change, fix, or control. But progress usually starts with one focus, one adjustment, one small step in the right direction. As Patrick Lencioni put it, *"If everything is important, then nothing is."*

Here's the challenge: it's not just about focusing on one thing—it's about focusing on the *right* thing. Not just what's urgent or easy, but what matters most. That's how real growth happens.

Don't feel like you have to change everything at once. Pick one practice, one idea, one truth. Work on it until it sticks. Then, when you've mastered it, come back and add another. That's how lasting change is built—one focus at a time.

Proverbs 4:25–27 says: *"Let your eyes look straight ahead; fix your gaze directly before you. Give careful thought to the paths for your feet and be steadfast in all your ways. Do not turn to the right or the left."*

What's the one thing God may be asking you to fix your eyes on today?

"One step at a time.
Baby steps are still steps."
—Toni Sorenson

Baby Steps

I sat in the chair at my orthodontist's office when Dr. Paul Gates informed me that I would be wearing rubber bands on my braces for the next nine months. As if it wasn't already humbling enough to be a 45-year-old man with a mouth full of braces, now I had to add rubber bands. They weren't just uncomfortable—they made my job as a keynote speaker even more challenging.

I asked Dr. Gates if he could tighten them a little more so we could speed things up. He smiled and shook his head. "There are no shortcuts," he said. "Moving teeth into the right position takes time. If you double up on rubber bands or make them too tight, you'll do more harm than good. The only way is to wear them consistently, day after day. Over time, they'll shift."

He was right. Nine months later, I saw the results. Not from one giant leap, but from the slow, steady pressure of tiny, daily adjustments.

That truth goes far beyond orthodontics. Whether in leadership, faith, or personal growth, meaningful change almost always happens gradually. We want instant transformation, but the reality is this: one small step forward is always better than standing still.

Research backs this up. James Clear, in his book *Atomic Habits*, says, *"Success is the product of daily habits, not once-in-a-lifetime transformations."* Neuroscience also shows that small, repeated actions literally rewire our brains over time, making change more sustainable.

The Bible echoes this principle of steady growth. Zechariah 4:10 says, *"Do not despise these small beginnings, for the Lord rejoices to see the work begin."* God often works through slow, unseen progress that eventually produces lasting fruit.

So, when you feel like change is too slow, remember this: baby steps are better than no steps. One rubber band at a time. One habit at a time. One choice at a time. That's how you shape the future.

Where in your life do you need to be patient with the process? And what's one baby step you can take today that your future self will thank you for?

"There's a whisper inside you...
it's saying it's time to kick it up a notch."
—Nick Ortner

Whirley Pop

Tracy and I love popcorn. In fact, our popcorn is so good we've been tempted to sneak it into the movie theater (no comment on whether we actually have).

One night, before a movie, I pulled out our Whirley Pop. I scooped in the butter-flavored coconut oil, measured out the kernels, sprinkled in the salt and secret movie-theater spice, and melted the butter in the microwave. I cranked the handle and waited for that magical sound—pop, pop, pop.

But nothing happened. The kernels just sat there. I kept turning, and thinking, *What's going on here? Is the corn expired? Did I break the Whirley Pop?* I even started rehearsing (in my head) the speech I'd give Tracy about why we'd have to switch to ice cream instead.

Then I realized the problem. I'd forgotten to turn up the heat. The oil was warm—but not hot enough to make anything happen. Once I cranked it up, the kernels started bursting like fireworks, and soon, we had the best popcorn on the planet.

This reminds me of a truth we can often forget. At times, we might be doing all the right things, but the results don't come because the heat isn't high enough. It's not about waiting longer—it's about turning up the energy, the effort, the intensity.

Think about it. Edison failed thousands of times before the light bulb worked. Lincoln lost election after election before finally stepping into the presidency. Colonel Sanders heard "no" over a thousand times before someone finally said yes to his secret chicken recipe. They didn't quit. They didn't coast. They turned up the heat.

Psychologist Angela Duckworth calls this *grit*—passion plus perseverance. Her research shows grit, not talent or luck, is the strongest predictor of long-term success. The people who keep cranking up the heat are the ones who pop. Spiritually, Paul puts it this way: *"Never be lacking in zeal, but keep your spiritual fervor, serving the Lord"* (Romans 12:11).

And here's another reminder I love: Popcorn cooks in the same pot, in the same oil, on the same stove—but the kernels don't all pop at the same time. Don't compare your timing to others. Your turn to pop is coming.

So, here's the takeaway: sometimes you don't need a new plan—you just need more passion. Maybe the effort you're giving now is warm, but not hot. Don't give up. Don't settle. Turn up the heat until you pop.

Where in your life do you need to add more energy, intensity, or focus—not just waiting, but leaning in harder?

"Drop by drop is the water pot filled.
Likewise, the wise one,
gathering it little by little,
fills oneself with good."

—Gautama Buddha

One Drop

Sometimes the hardest part of any task is just getting started.

That's where the "one drop" concept comes in.

The idea is simple: instead of trying to tackle the entire ocean, you just start with a drop. Do one push-up. Write one sentence. Read one verse. Take one step out the door. You don't need the whole plan—you just need the first drop.

This concept isn't new. Arthur Ashe encouraged us: *"Start where you are. Use what you have. Do what you can."* Thousands of years earlier, Confucius observed: *"The man who moves a mountain begins by carrying away small stones."* Big progress begins with small beginnings.

Behavioral researcher BJ Fogg expands on this in *Tiny Habits*: *"When something is tiny, it's easy to do—which means you don't need to rely on the unreliable nature of motivation."* We even see this principle in Scripture. Zechariah 4:10 says, *"Do not despise these small beginnings, for the Lord rejoices to see the work begin."* God delights in the first drop—the first prayer, the first act of obedience, the first small step in faith.

I had to lean on this when I walked the Camino. Instead of worrying about 500 miles, I didn't focus on Santiago—I just aimed for the next village. One step at a time. I applied this concept again while writing this book. The thought of drafting hundreds of pages felt overwhelming—so I started with one page. Drop by drop, those pages became this book.

Even Dr. Seuss understood this. In 1960, he wrote *Green Eggs and Ham* using only 50 different words—9 of them one syllable. Why? To prove you could do something great by keeping it simple. Sam-I-Am's persistence shows the same lesson: *"Try them, try them, and you may."* Just take the first bite, the first try, the first drop.

Here's the magic: once you start, momentum takes over. Psychologists call this the *Zeigarnik Effect*—the tendency of our brains to stay engaged with unfinished tasks. In other words, starting creates its own pull. That first drop not only makes the next step easier, it also helps us push past procrastination and actually build new habits.

Big things happen one drop at a time. It's not about the grand beginning—it's about the brave one. What's your "drop"?

What's a tiny step you can take today—so small you can't talk yourself out of it? What's one action that your future self will thank you for starting right now?

"Your life does not get better by chance;
it gets better by change."
—Jim Rohn

Wheel of Change

As we come to the end of this journey together, the question becomes simple—but not easy: What will you do with what you've learned?

Stories inspire. Insights encourage. But real change happens when reflection turns into action.

That's why I want to close with something practical—something you can return to long after you've finished this book: The Wheel of Change. It's a simple tool for reflection and decision-making, almost like a personal inventory with direction.

The Wheel of Change was developed by Marshall Goldsmith, one of the world's leading executive coaches and author of *What Got You Here Won't Get You There*. He created it to help leaders evaluate what needs to change in order to grow. But this tool isn't just for CEOs—it's for anyone who wants to live with greater purpose, joy, and mindfulness.

The Wheel has four quadrants: Keep, Let Go, Accept, and Create.

- **Keep.** What's already working in your life? What brings you peace, energy, or purpose? Maybe it's your morning walk, a weekly phone call with a friend, or a quiet moment with coffee and Scripture. Identify it, name it, and protect it. As Paul writes in 1 Thessalonians 5:21, *"Hold on to what is good."*
- **Let Go.** This is often the hardest—but also the most freeing. What's weighing you down or stealing your peace? A grudge, a fear, a habit, or maybe even an identity that no longer serves you. Hebrews 12:1 encourages us to *"throw off everything that hinders and the sin that so easily entangles, and run with perseverance the race marked out for us."* Letting go isn't about giving up—it's about making room for something better.
- **Accept.** There are things in life we simply cannot change—a diagnosis, a season of waiting, or the way someone else chooses to act. Acceptance doesn't mean approval; it means peace. It's choosing to release the battle with reality. Paul modeled this in Philippians 4:11–12 when he said, *"I have learned to be content whatever the circumstances."*
- **Create.** This is where possibility lives. What new habit, boundary, project, or dream is God nudging you toward? What's been stirring in your heart that you haven't acted on yet? Ephesians 2:10 encourages us, *"We are God's handiwork, created in Christ Jesus to do good works, which*

> *God prepared in advance for us to do."* Create is about stepping boldly into those good works.

Take a few minutes to sketch out your own wheel. Write down one or two things in each quadrant. Don't overcomplicate it. Don't try to fix everything. Just take one mindful step in each direction.

This is where reflection turns into movement.

This is where the Japanese concept of *Kaizen* comes in. Kaizen means "good change" or "continuous improvement". It's the practice of making small, steady steps that compound into meaningful change. Just like the stories we've walked through in this book—whether it's one drop at a time, keeping your left elbow straight, or practicing baby steps—it's about progress, not perfection.

Here's the truth: you don't have to overhaul your life in one sweeping gesture. Real change happens when you keep what's good, let go of what holds you back, accept what you can't control, and create what God is calling you into next.

So, here's your invitation: take the wheel, pray over it, write in it, and let it guide you. Choose one faithful movement at a time. Because small, mindful steps really do lead to lasting change.

And as you move forward, let me leave you with this:

I believe in you. I believe in your ability to push the door open to a more joyful, more prayerful, more thankful you. If you've read the stories, reflected on the lessons, and wrestled with the questions, now comes the hard part: living it out. You'll need to be dedicated, consistent, and willing to put in the work, if you want to experience the rewards and blessings on the other side.

It won't be easy. But it *will* be worth it.

Acknowledgements

FIRST AND FOREMOST, I give all glory and honor to God. Without His grace and guidance, this book would not exist. He is the source of my joy, the reason for my prayers, and the foundation of my thankfulness. Every page reflects His goodness in my life.

To my amazing wife, Tracy - thank you for your unwavering support, constant encouragement, and endless love. Your belief in me has been a steady light through every step of this journey. This book is as much yours as it is mine.

I also want to express deep gratitude to the countless teachers in my life. My mom and dad, who laid the foundation of faith, values, and perseverance in me. And to the many people I've encountered over my 35-year career - colleagues, clients, mentors, and team members - thank you for the lessons, the inspiration, and the shared experiences that have shaped me personally and professionally.

To all those who have supported me with encouragement, humor, and prayers - thank you. May this book bless you as you have blessed me.

About Kevin

KEVIN KARSCHNIK is a keynote speaker and author who inspires audiences with messages of positivity, gratitude, and faith. Drawing on more than 30 years as an entrepreneur, he blends wisdom, humor, and heart into every message he shares.

A kidney transplant recipient, Kevin's life is a testament to resilience and grace. He has faced adversity with a deep trust in God and a commitment to living each day with purpose. His journey fuels his passion for helping others discover the strength found in faith, the peace found in prayer, and the joy found in gratitude.

A devoted husband to Tracy, and proud father to Kip and Kait, Kevin values faith, family, and meaningful connections above all. Whether he's inspiring others through a keynote presentation, the written word, or simply sharing a moment of encouragement, Kevin's mission is clear: to help others live joyfully, pray faithfully, and give thanks always.

Learn more about Kevin's speaking and writing at

www.KevinKarschnik.com

Made in the USA
Coppell, TX
27 June 2026

83161545R00125